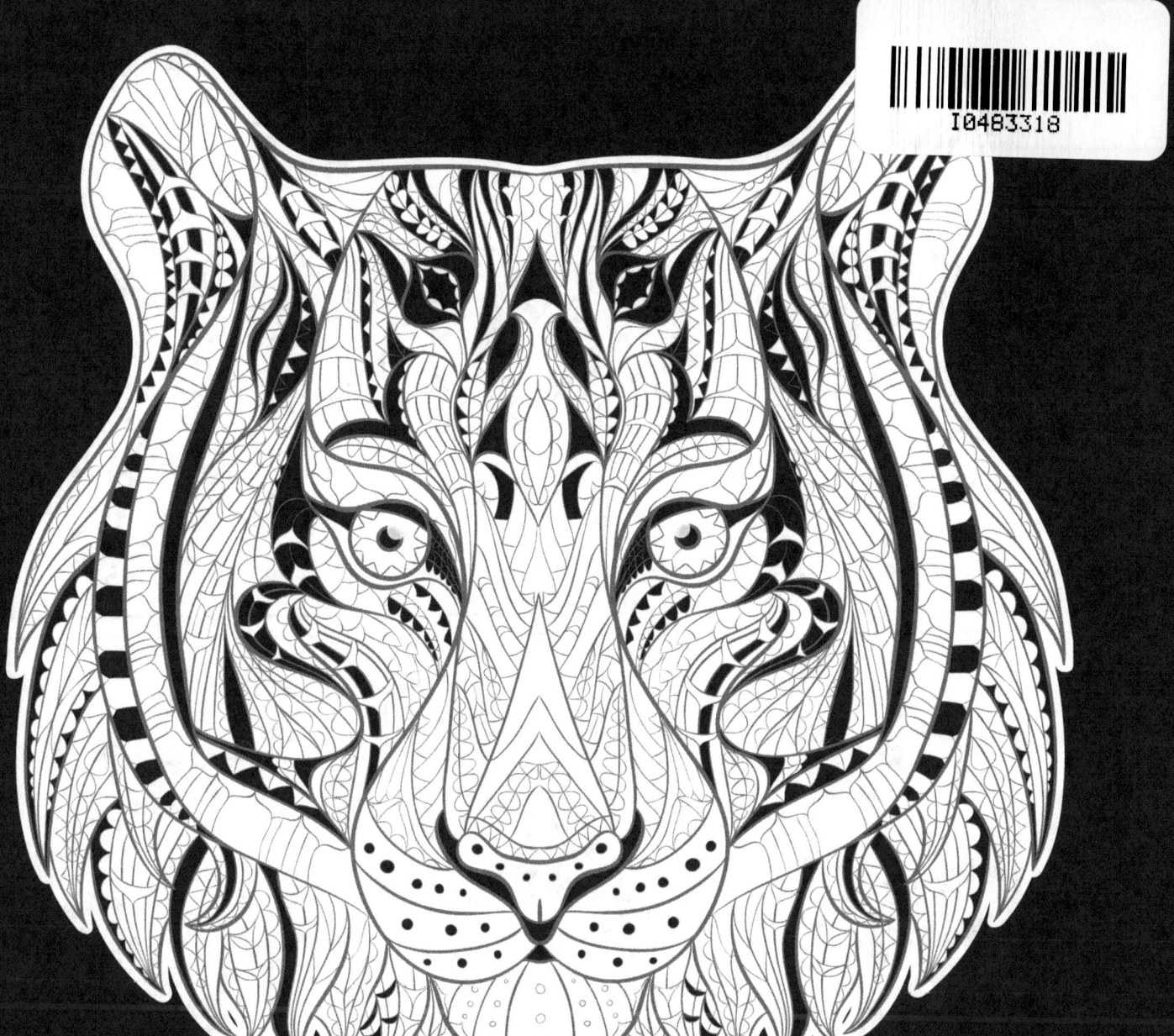

# TIGER
## COLORING BOOK
## FOR ADULTS

▲ ART THERAPY COLORING

# Preview of Coloring Pages

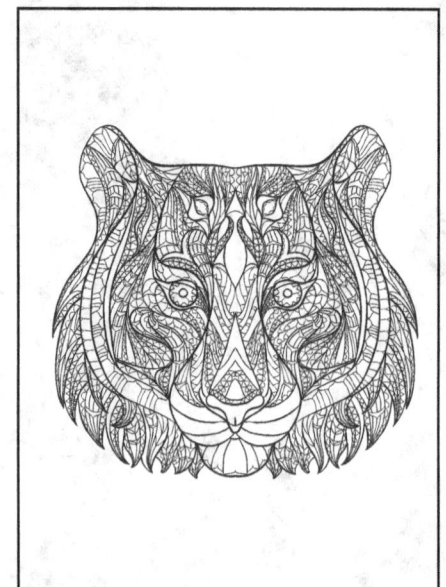
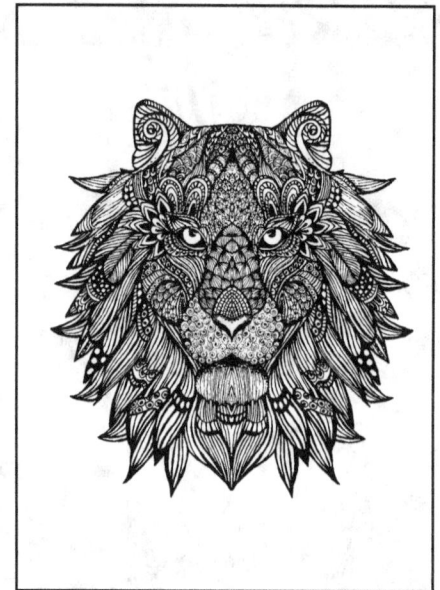
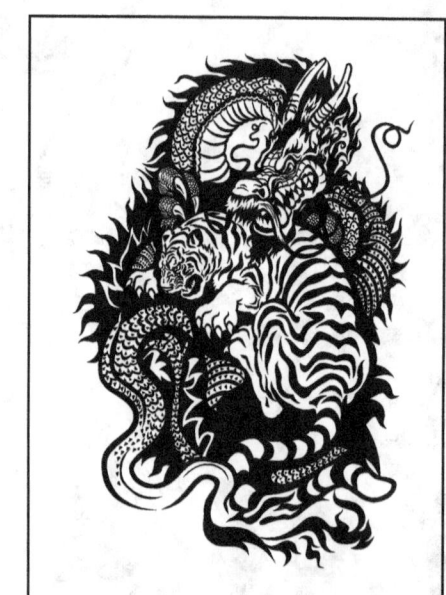
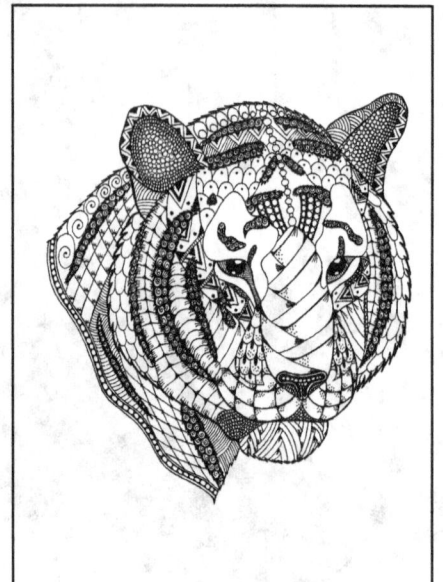
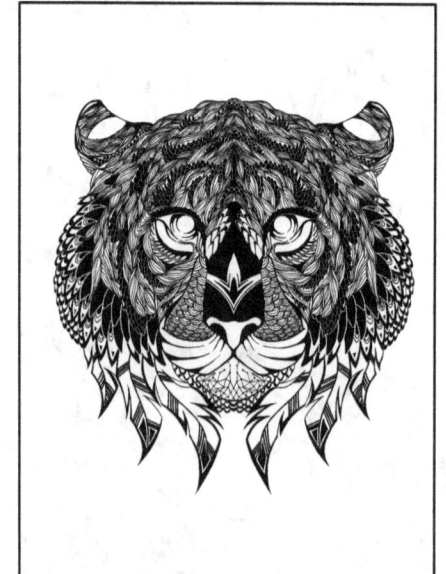
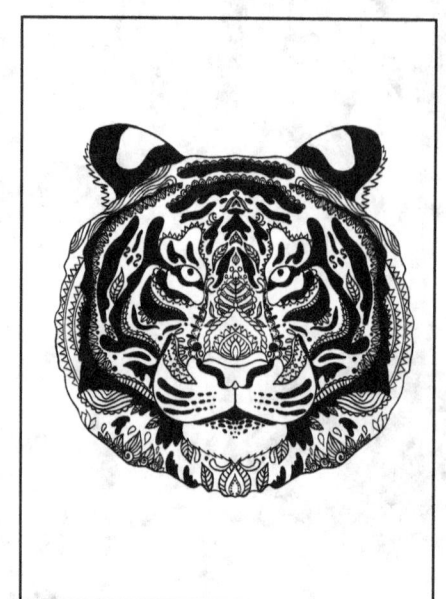
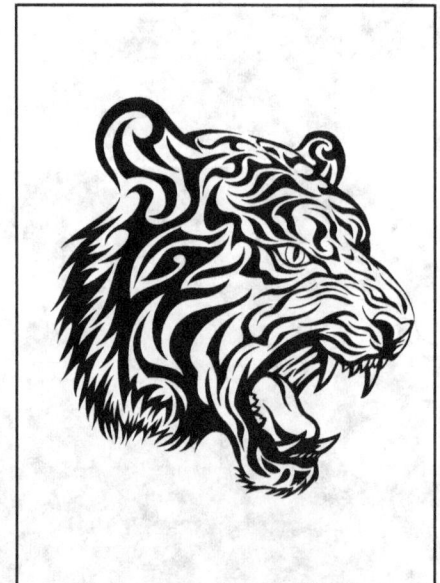
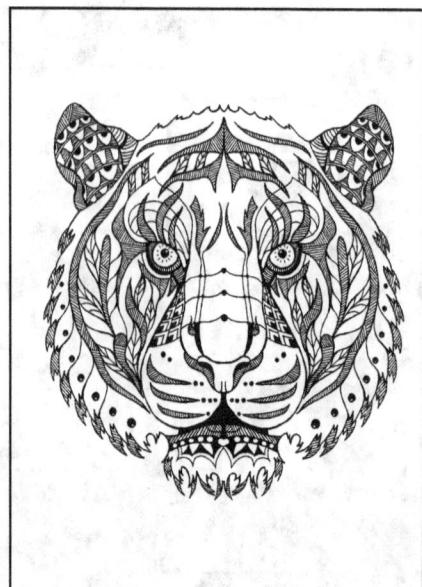
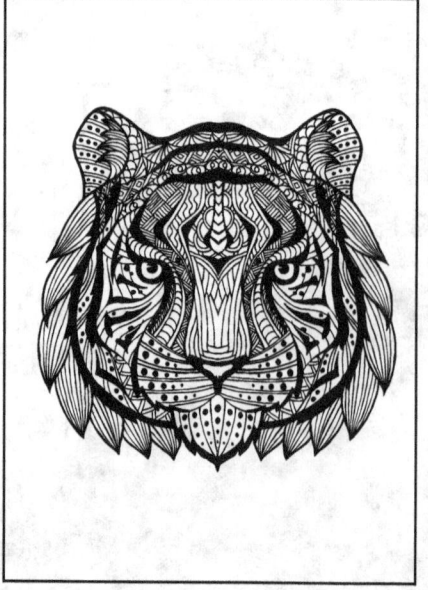

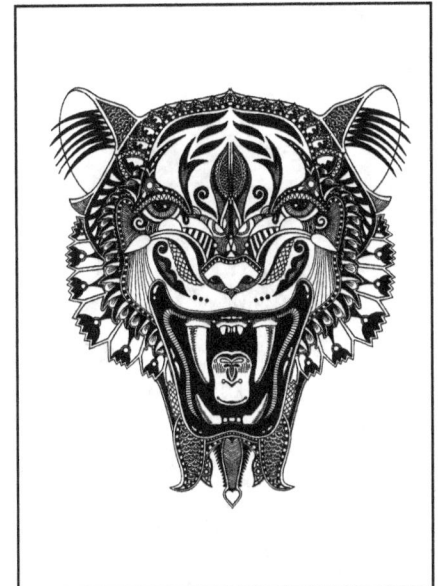
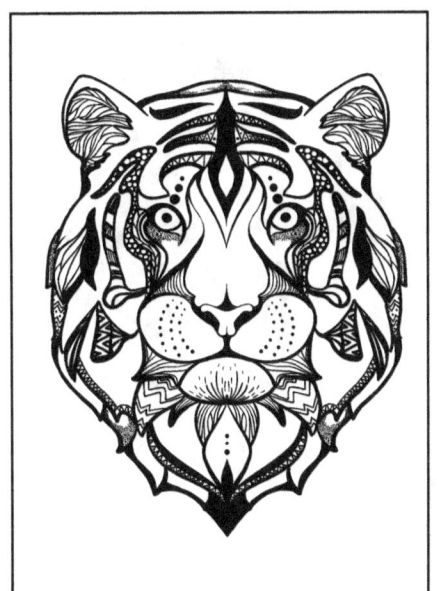
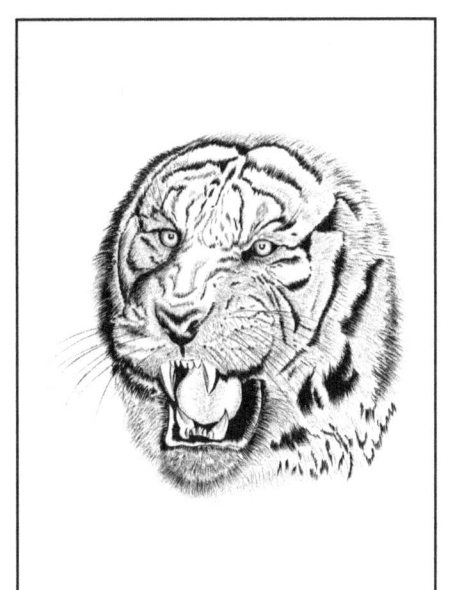
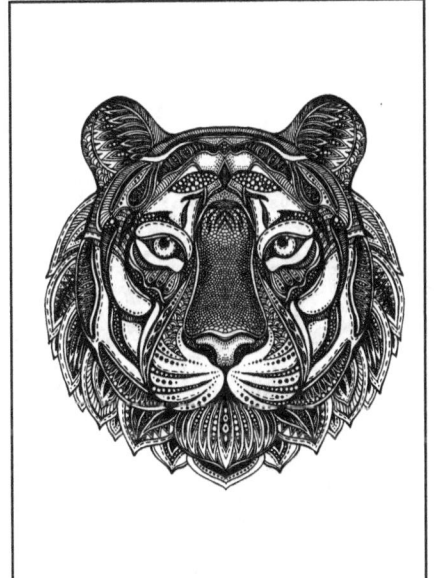
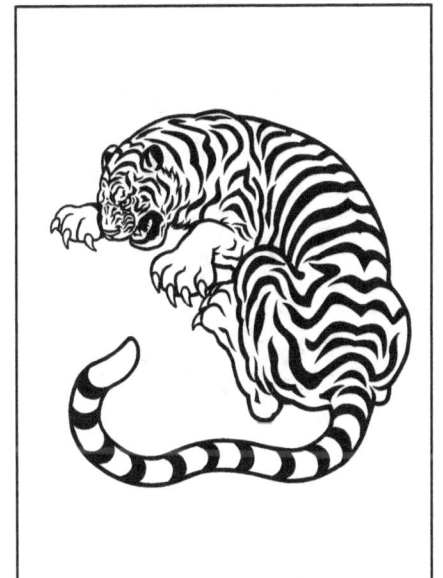
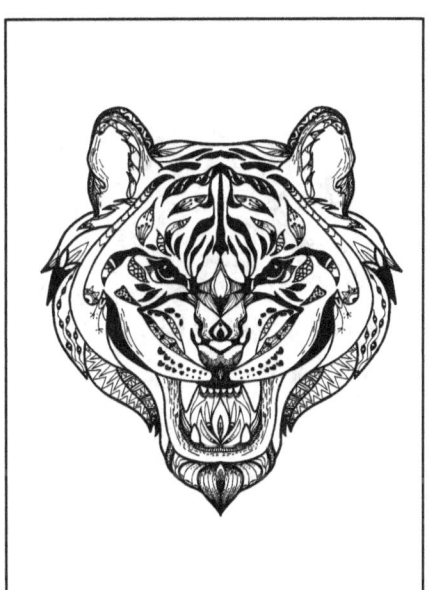
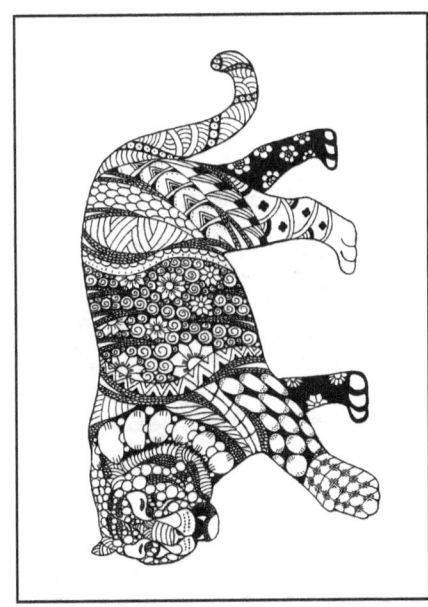
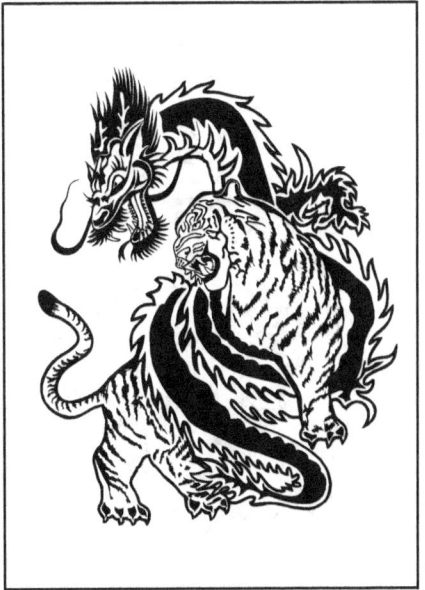
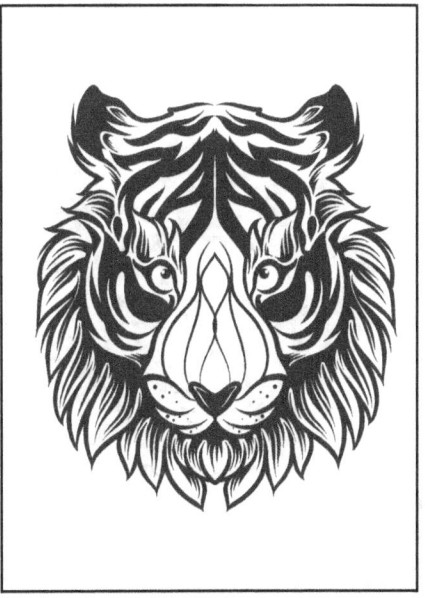

# Preview of Coloring Pages

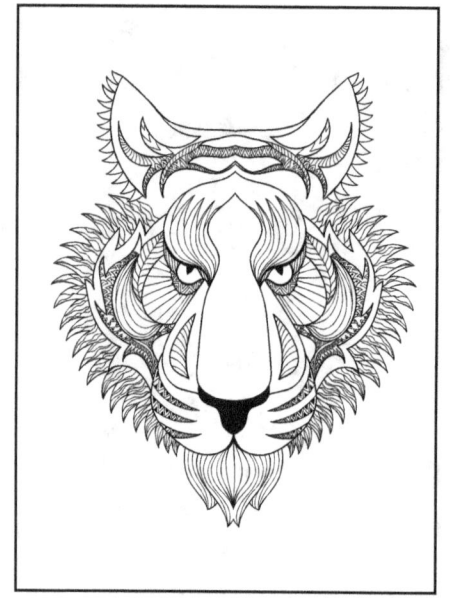
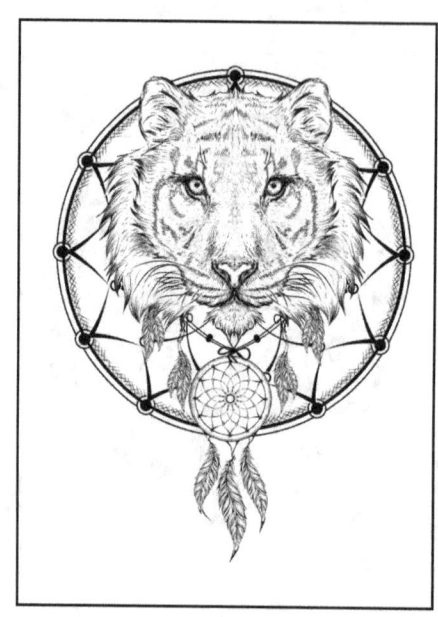
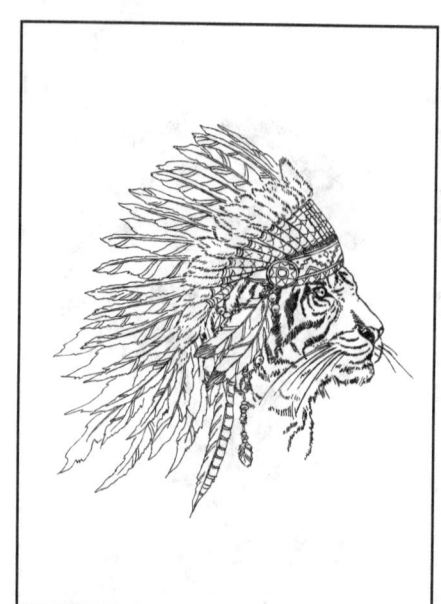
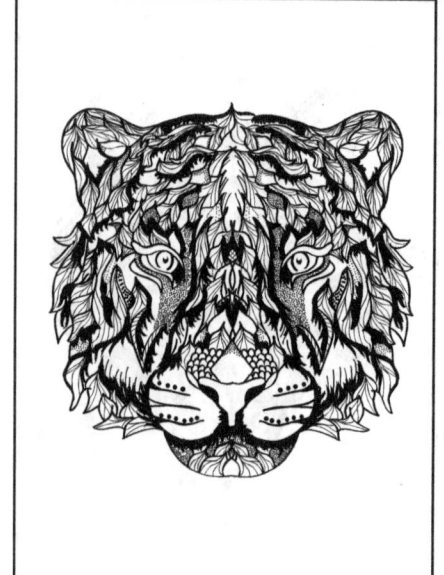
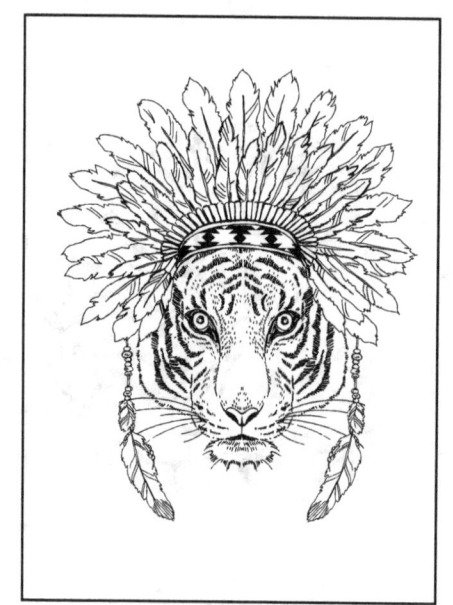
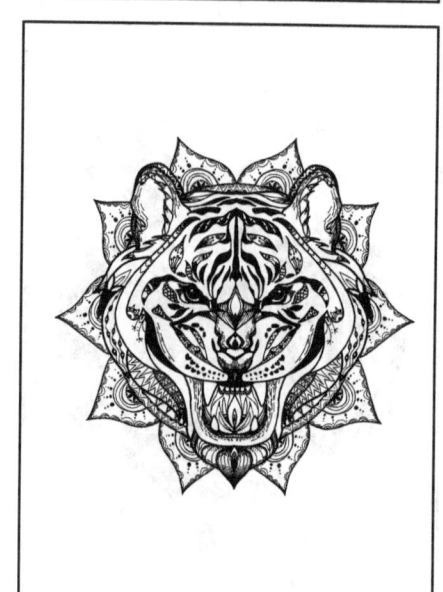
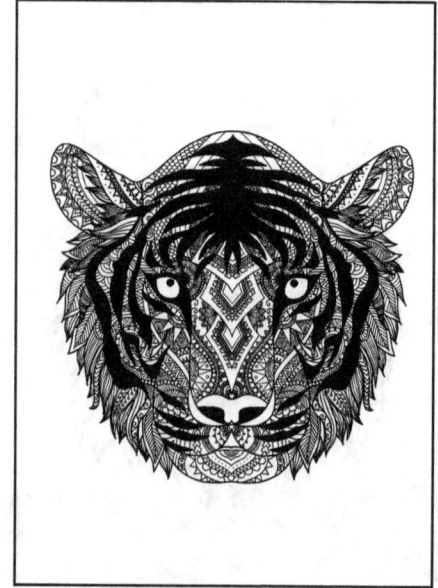
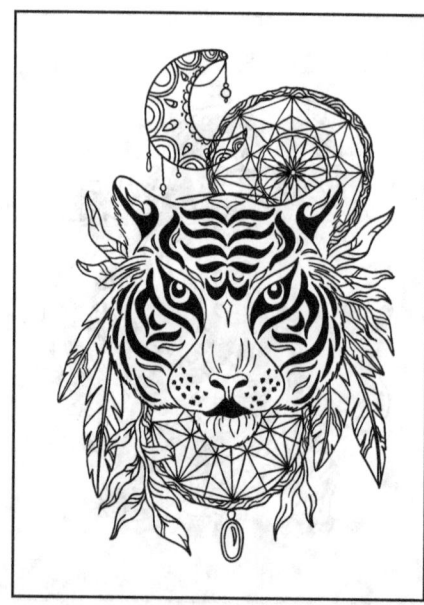
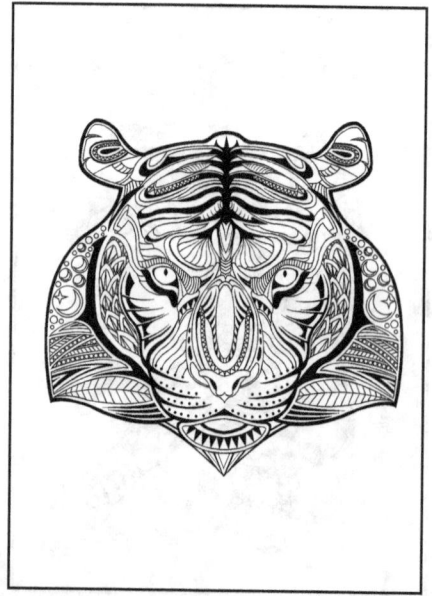

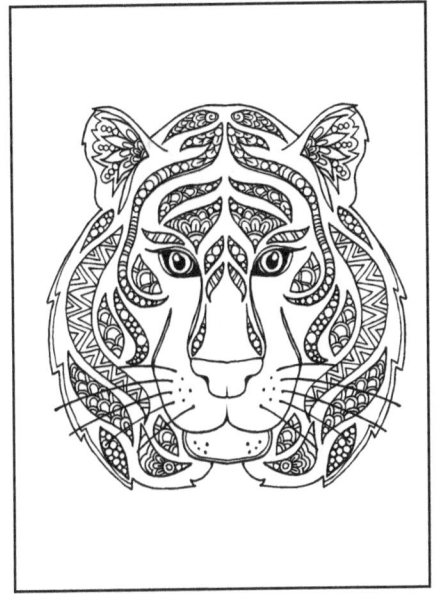
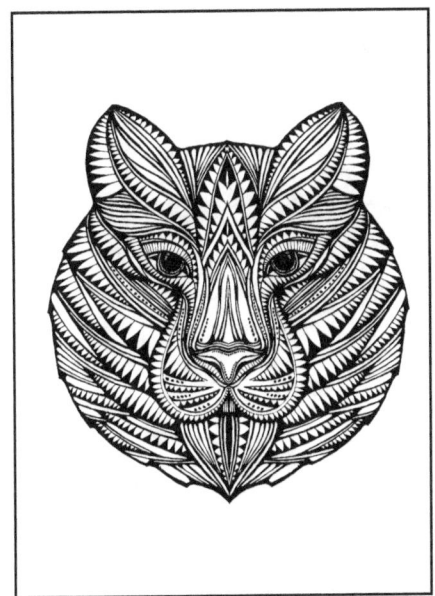
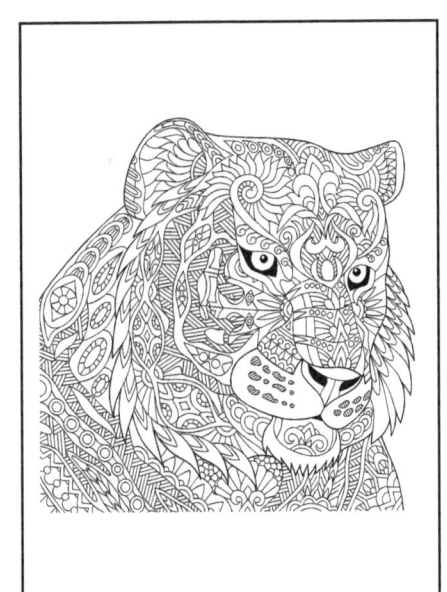
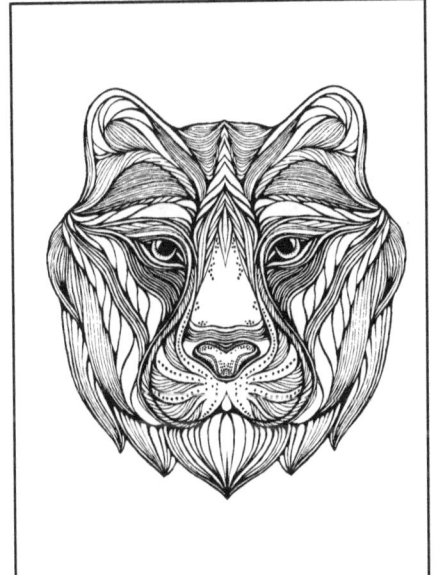
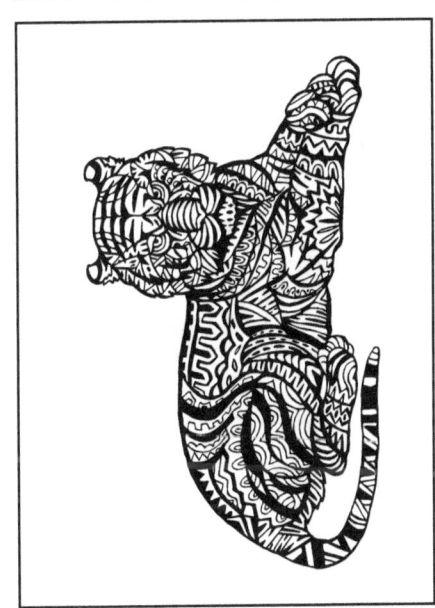
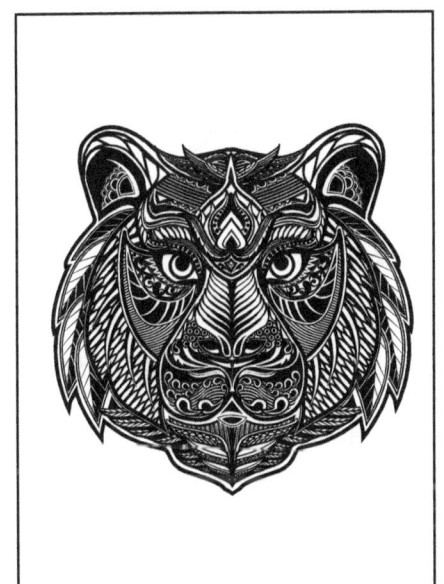
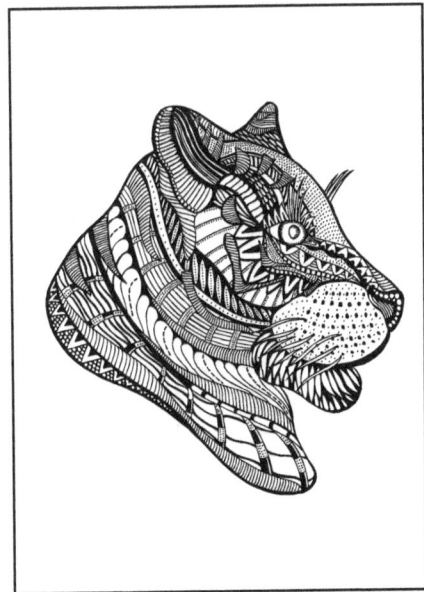
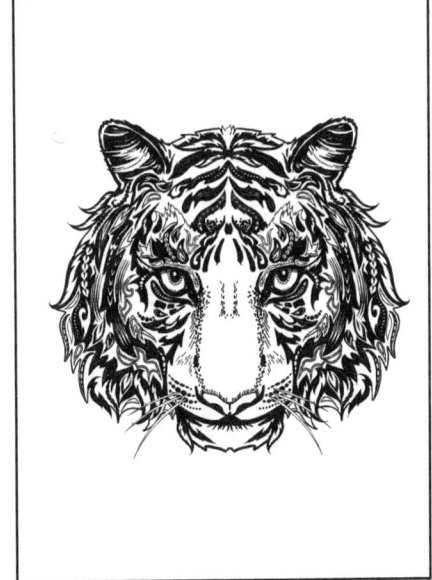
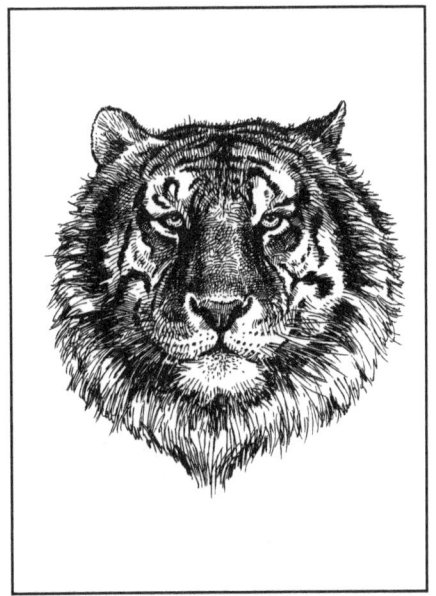

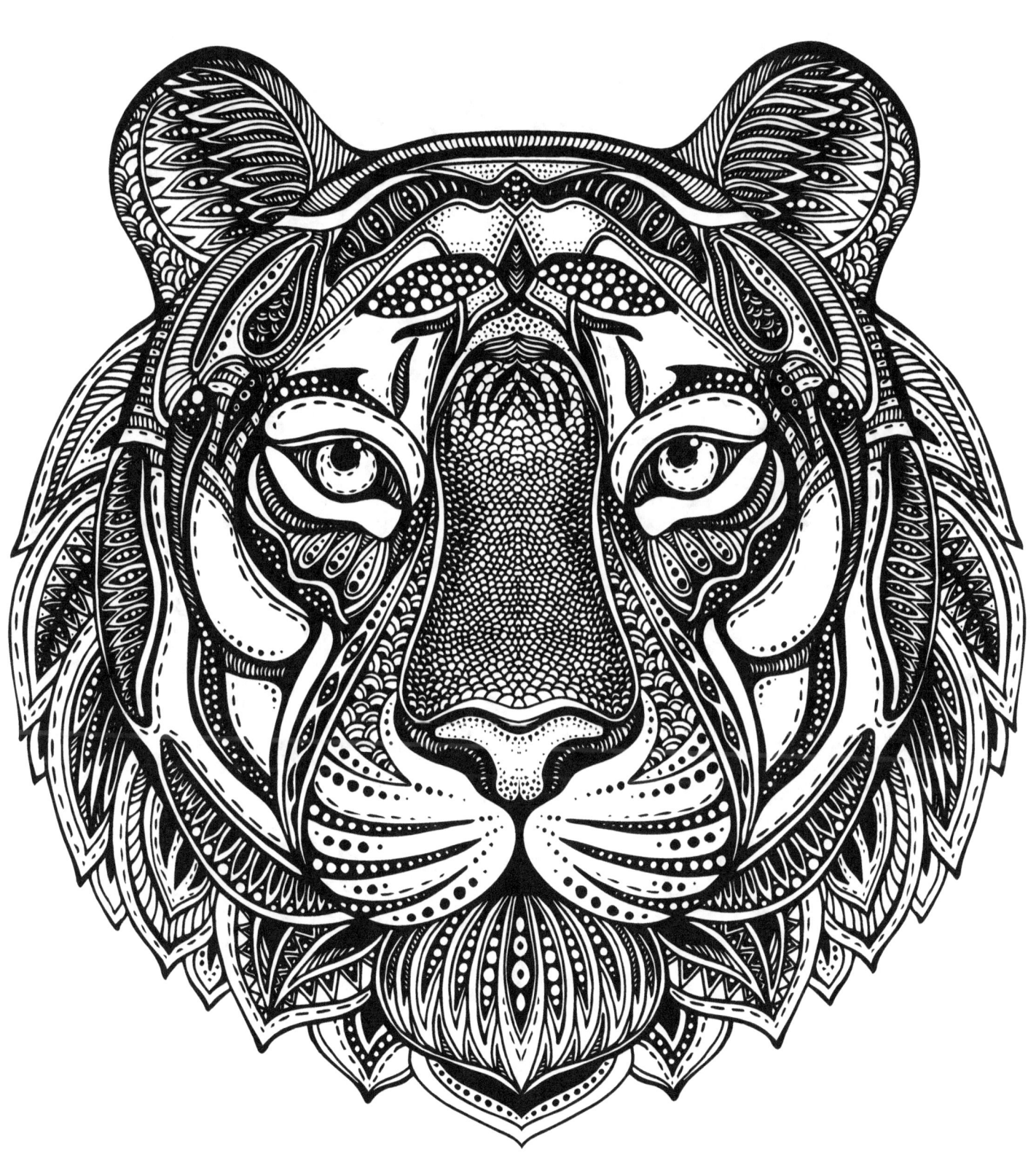

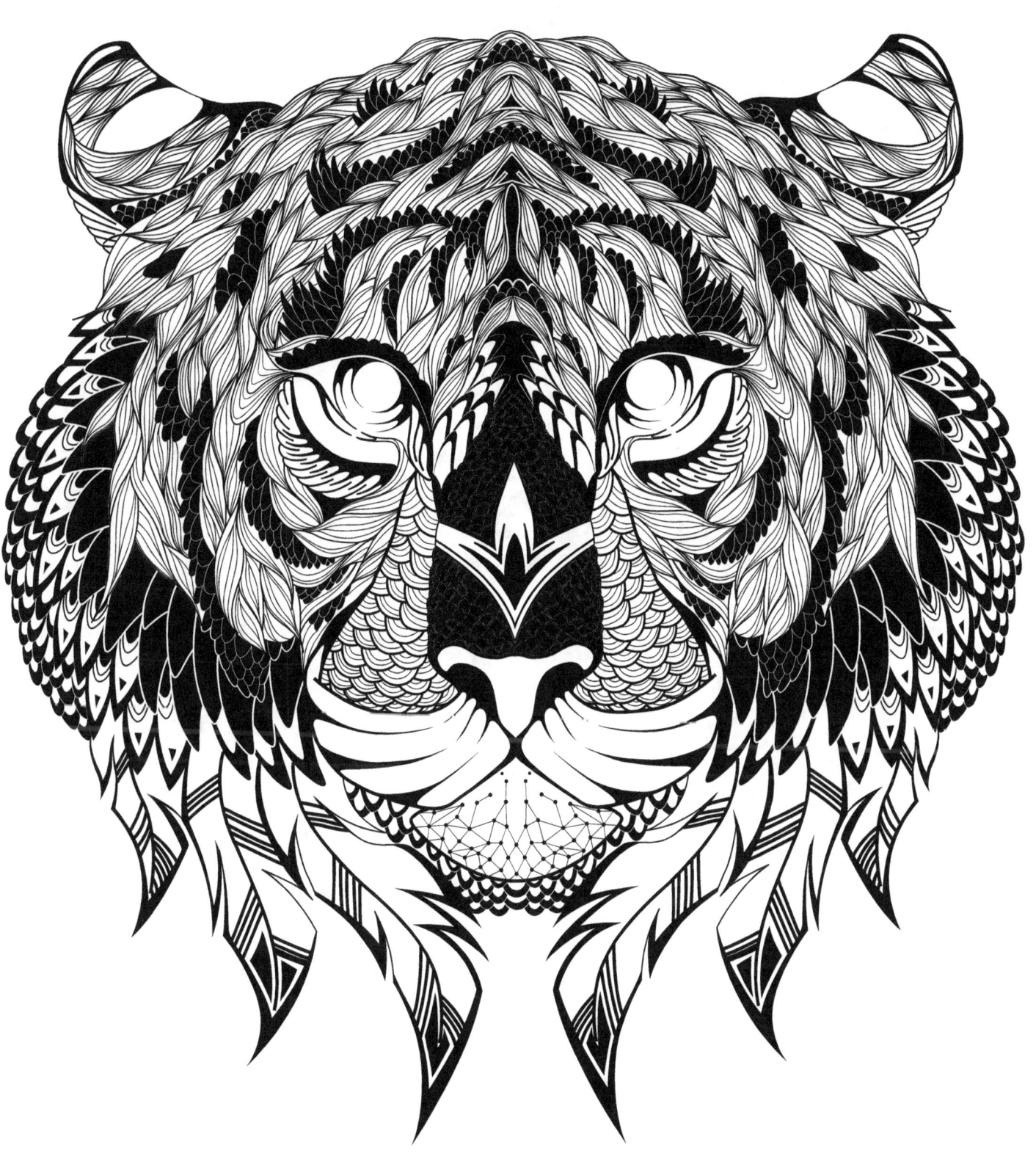

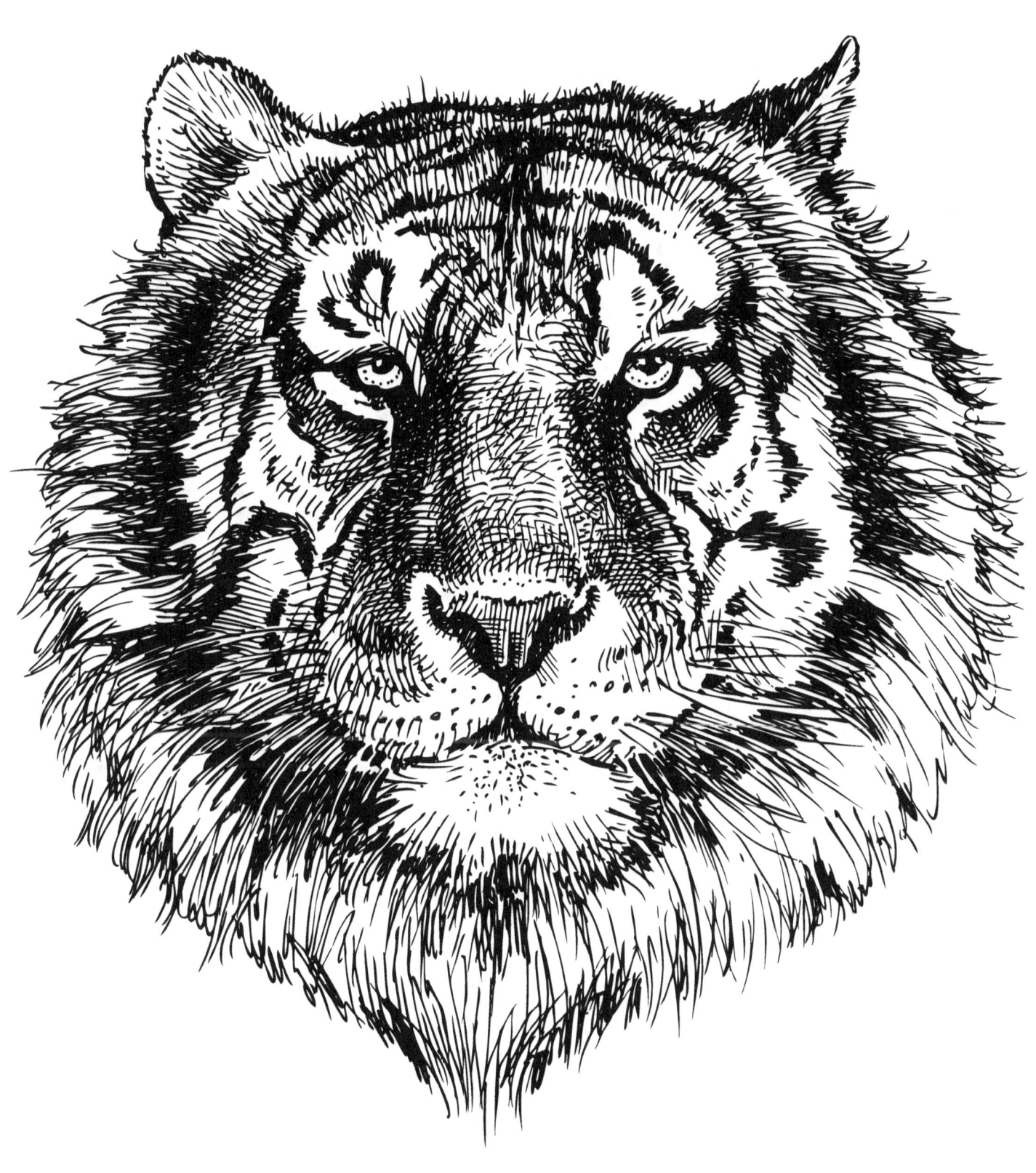

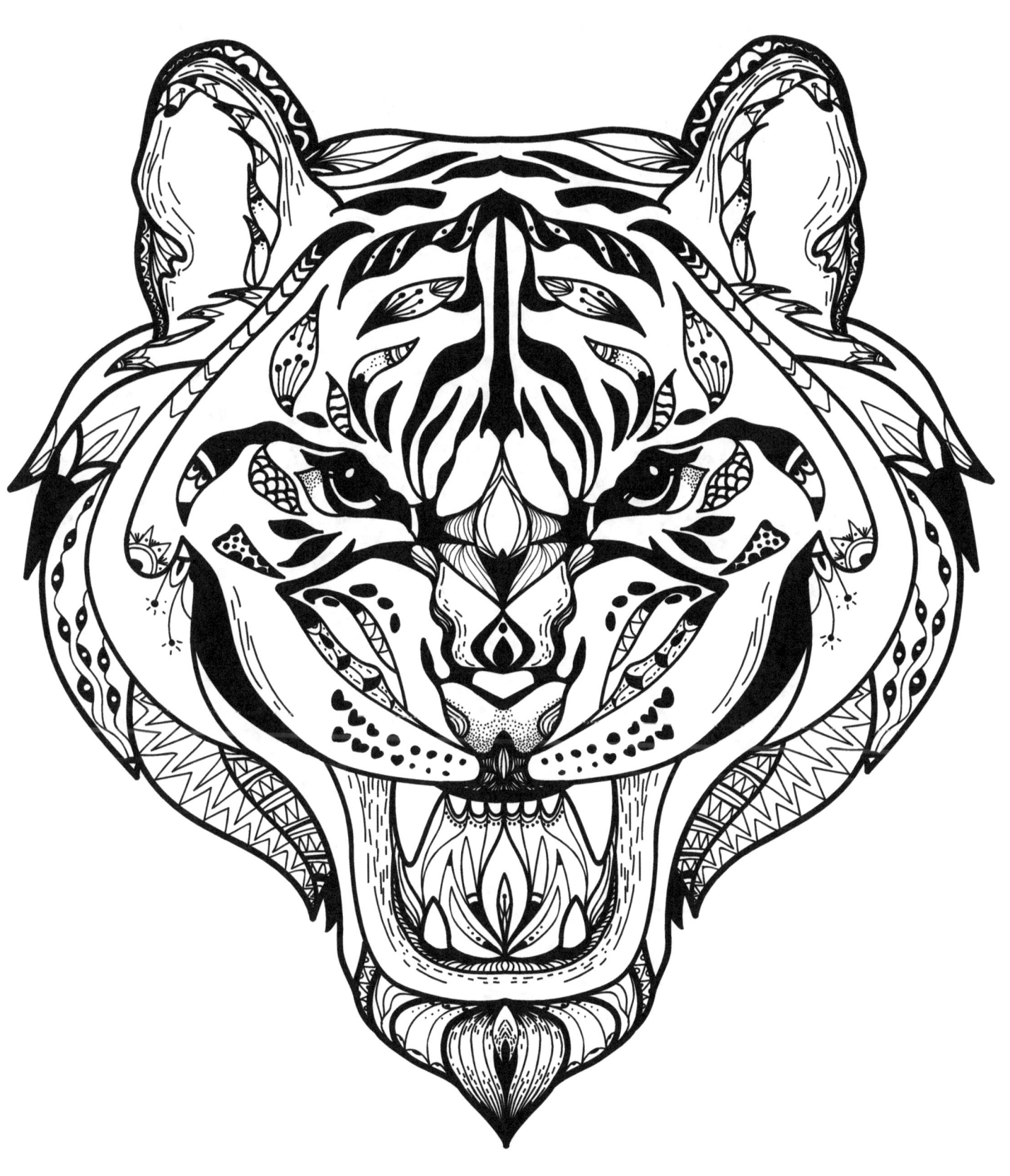

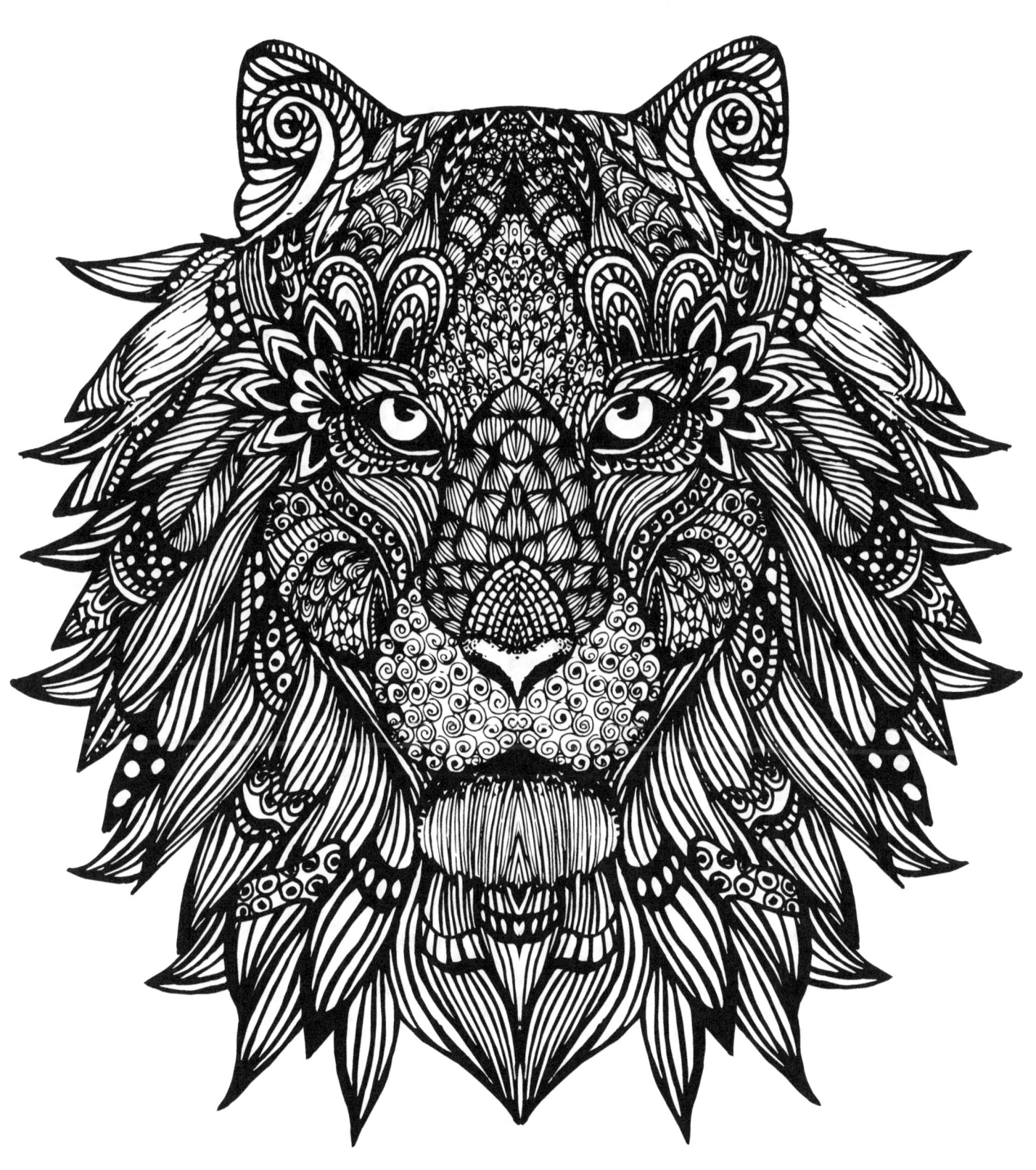

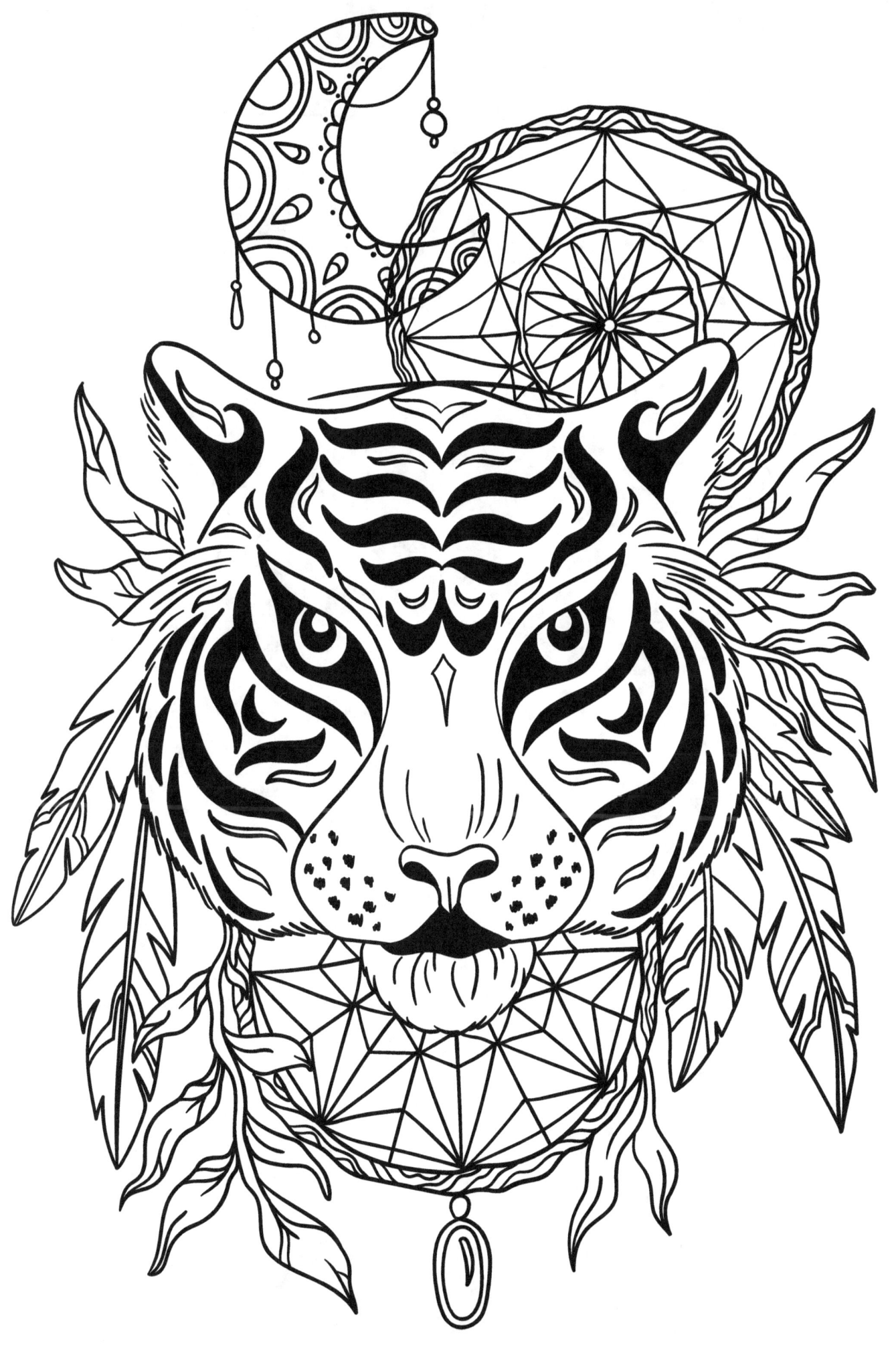

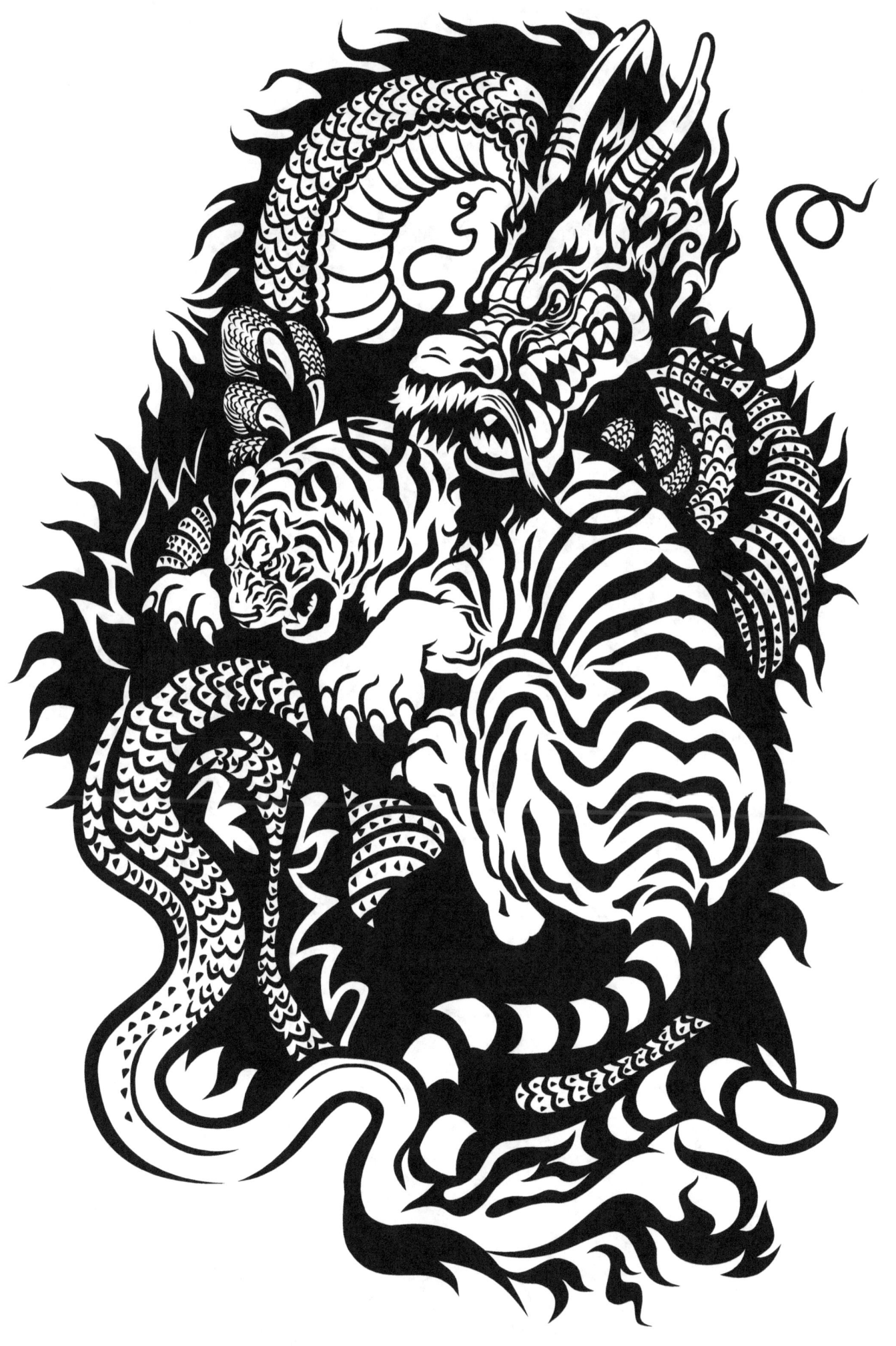

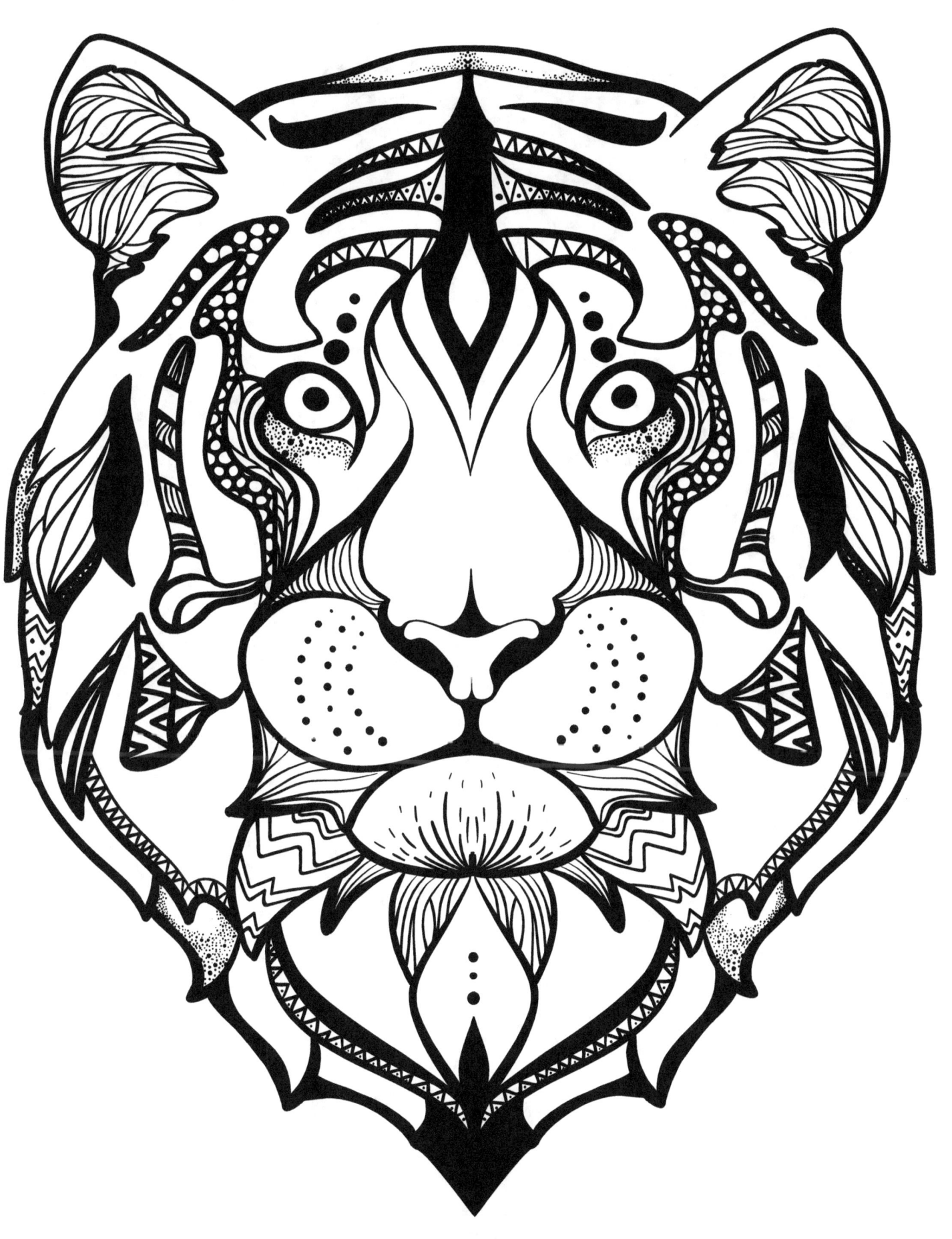

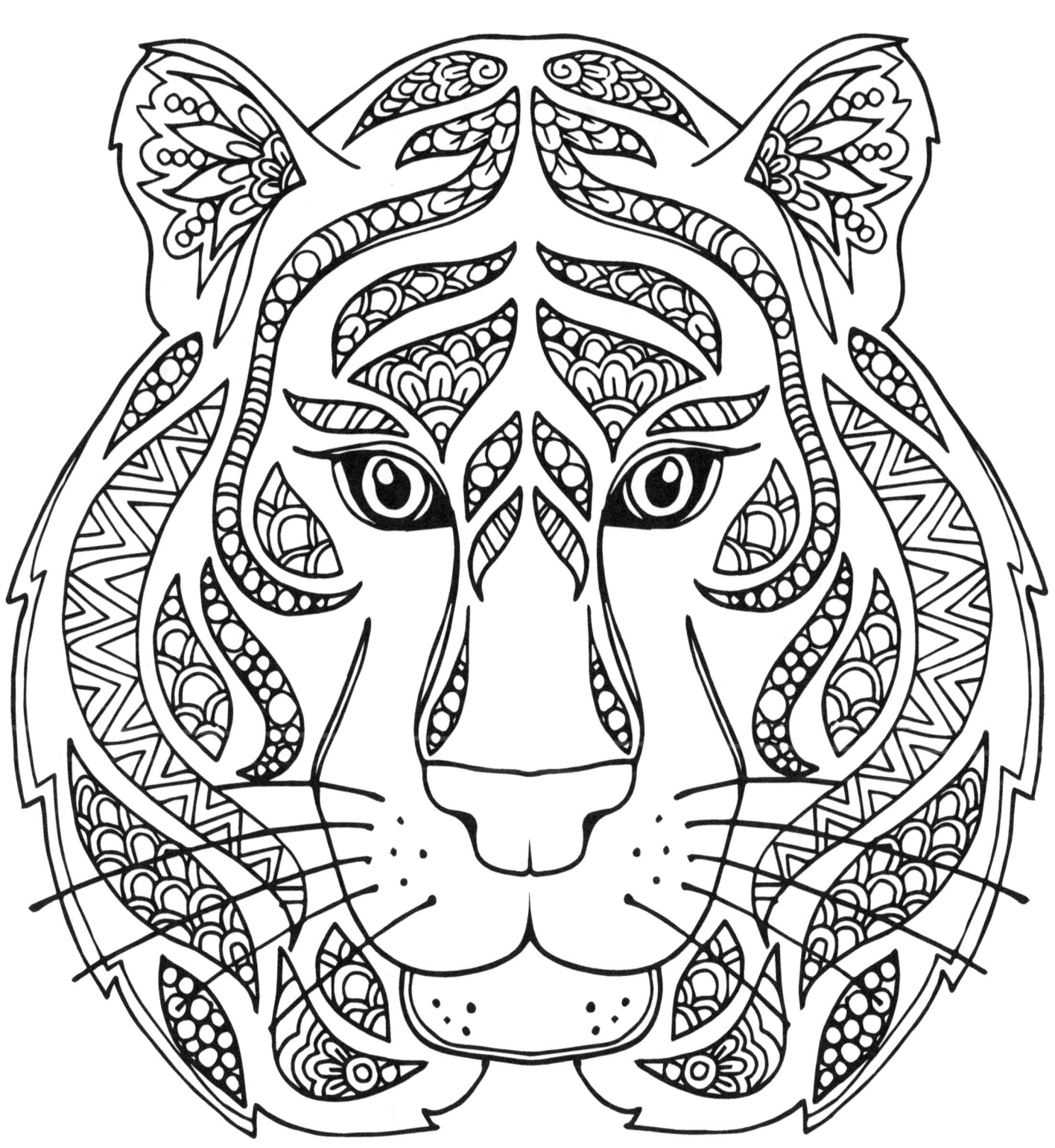

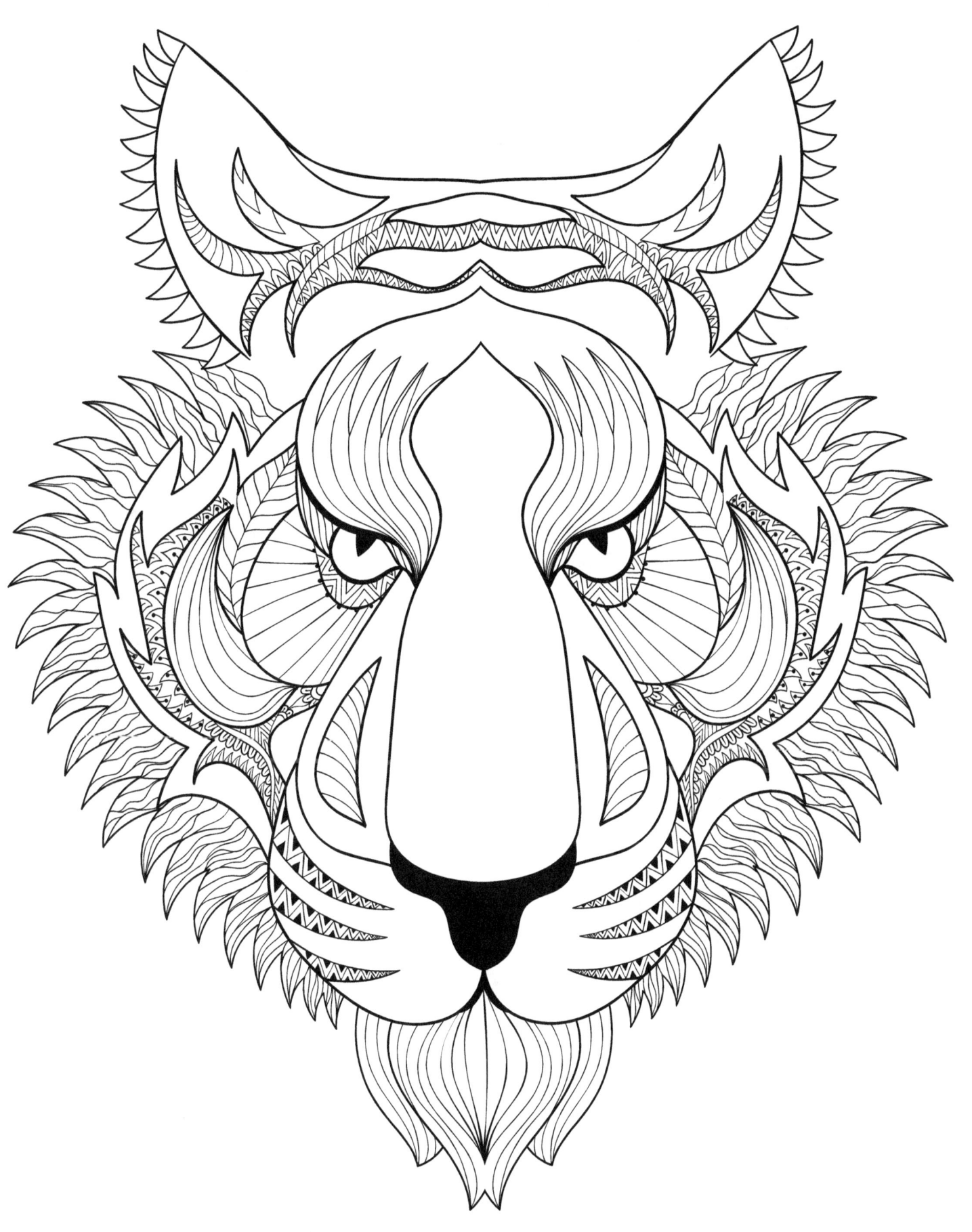

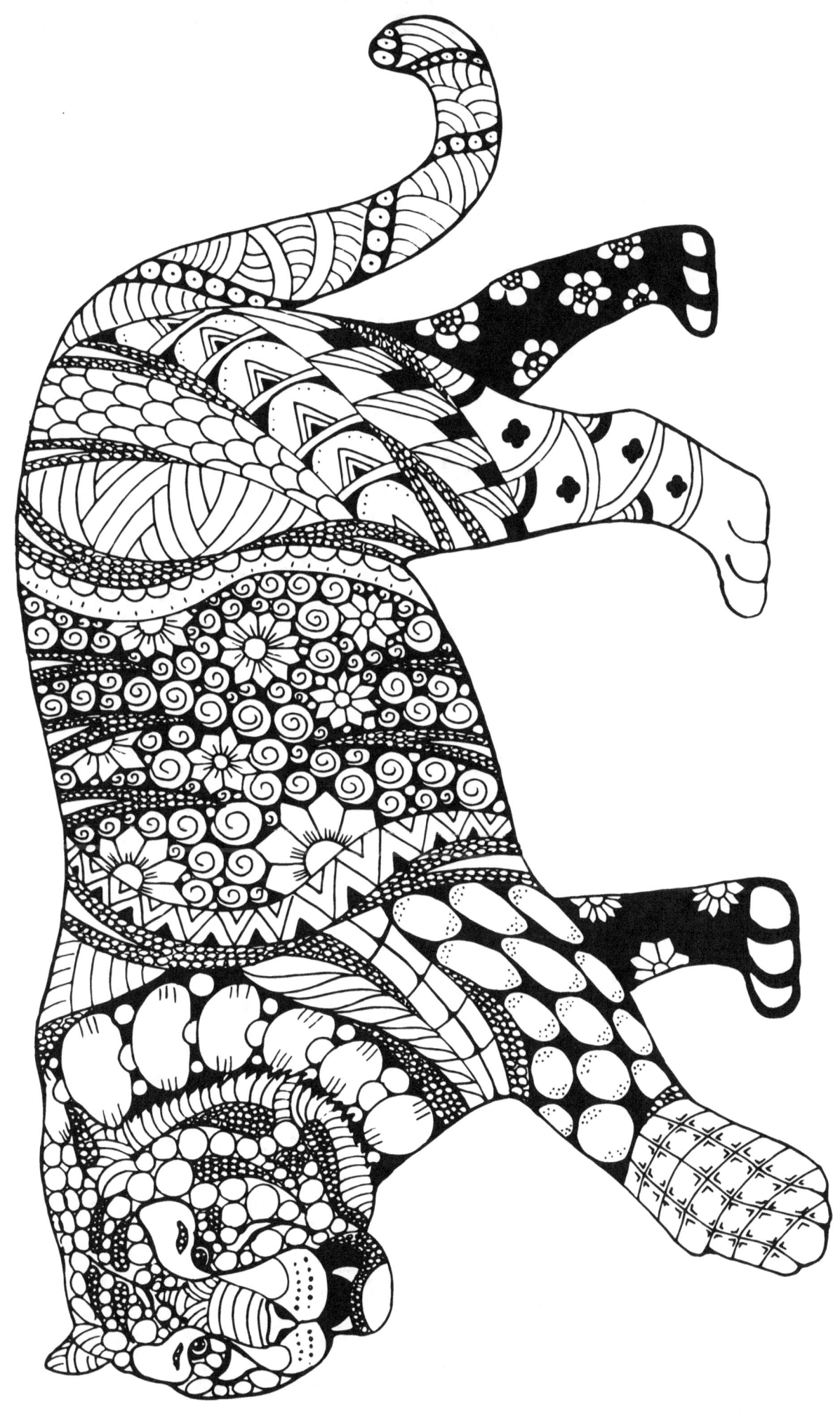

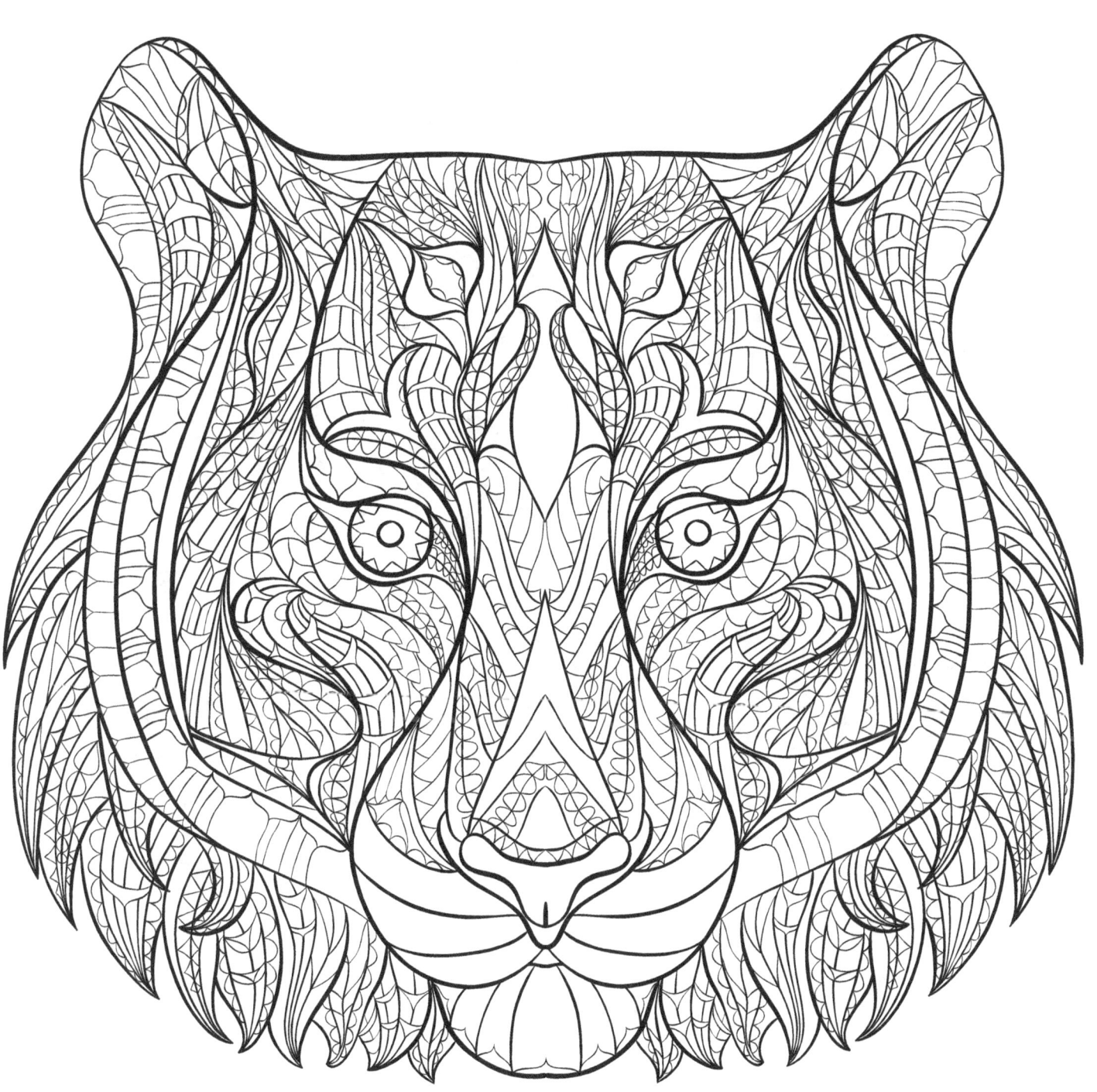

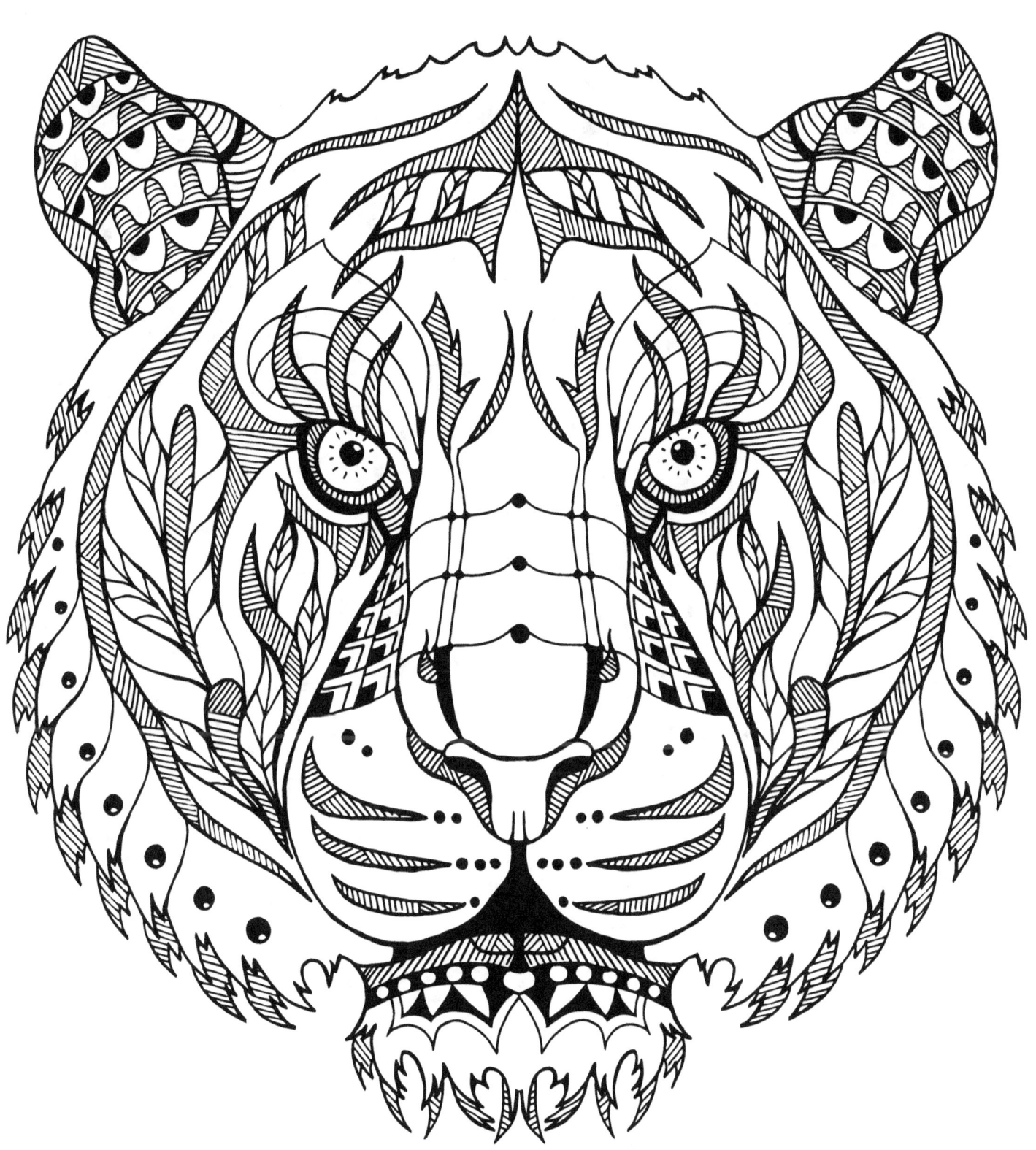

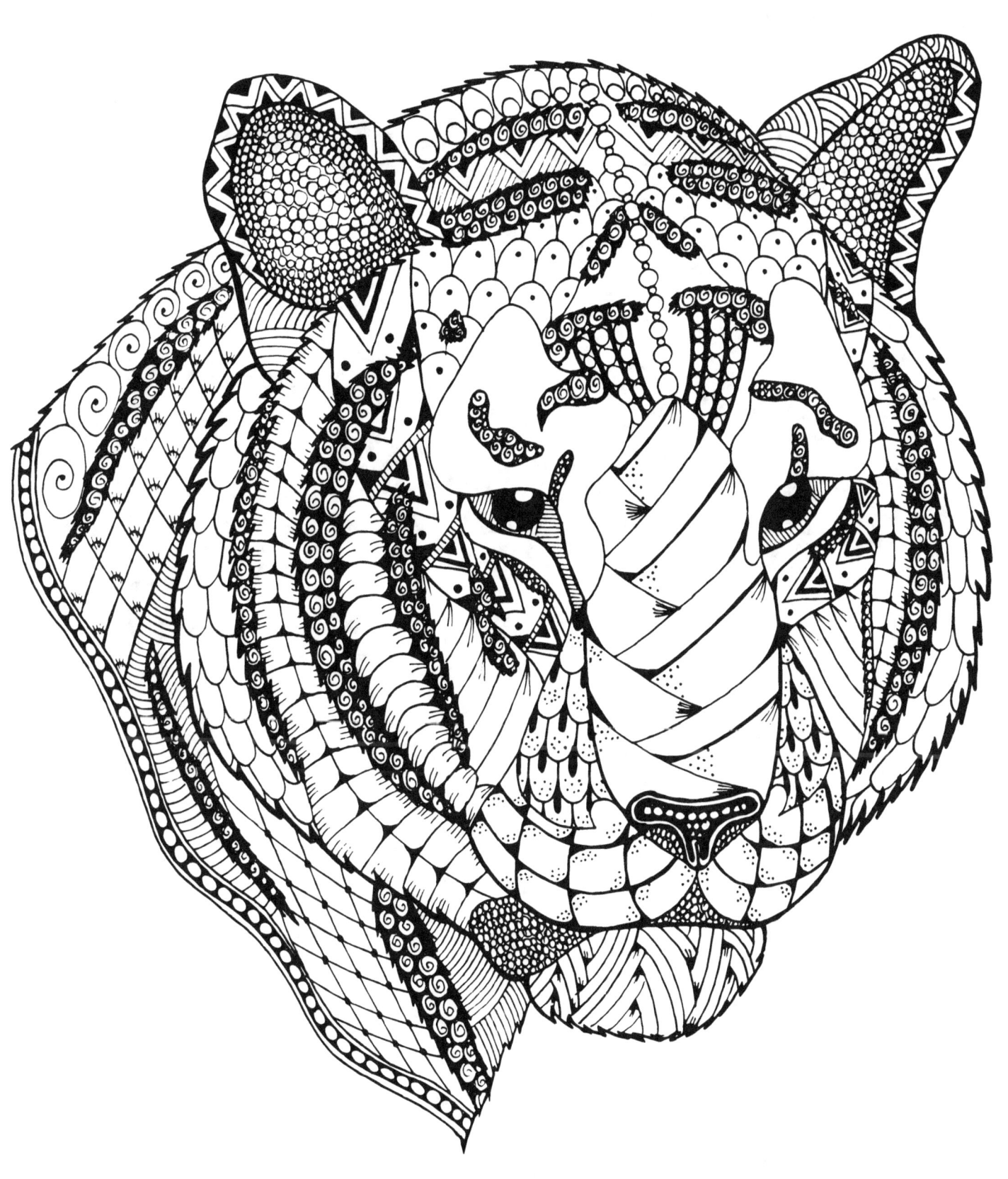

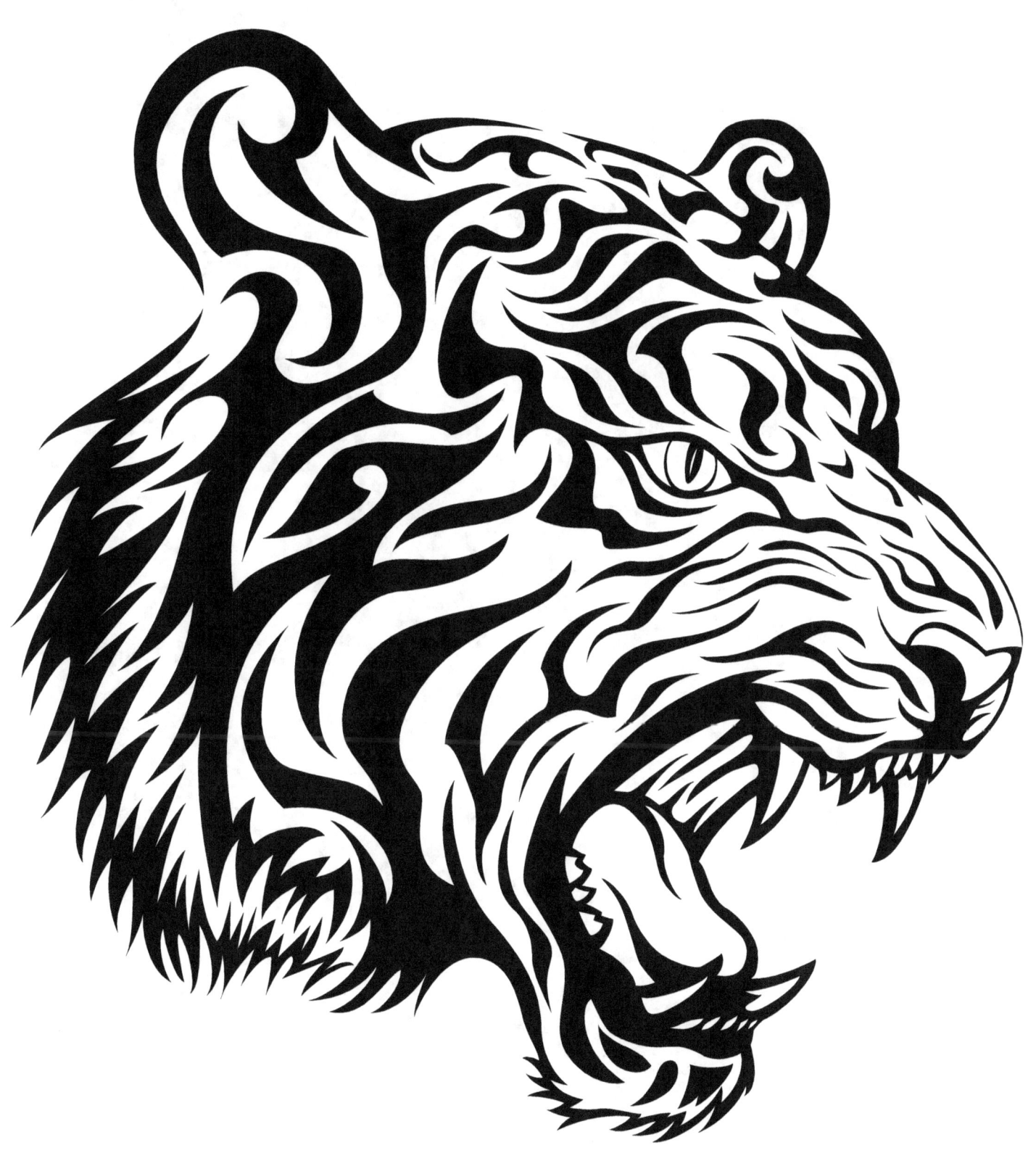

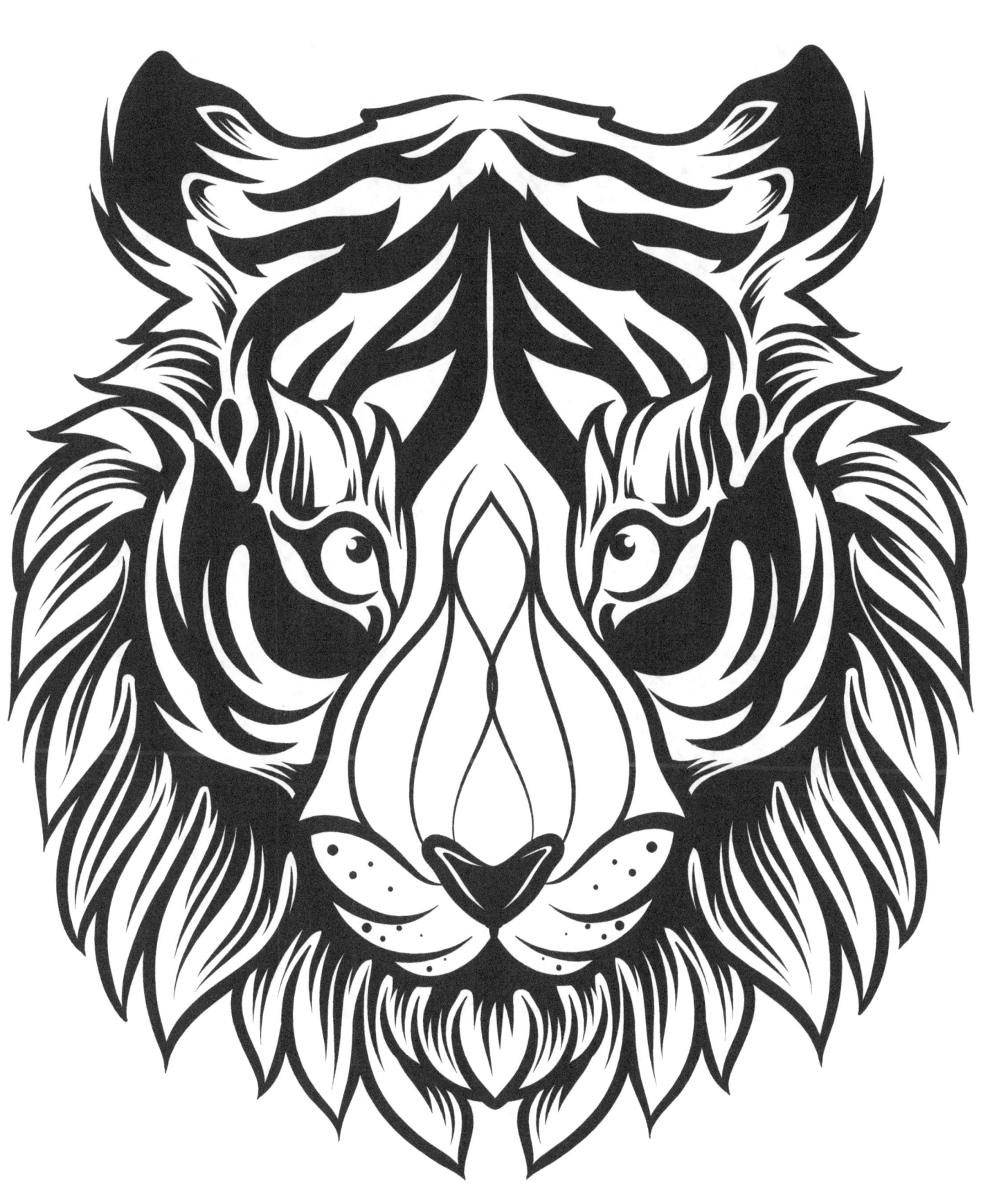

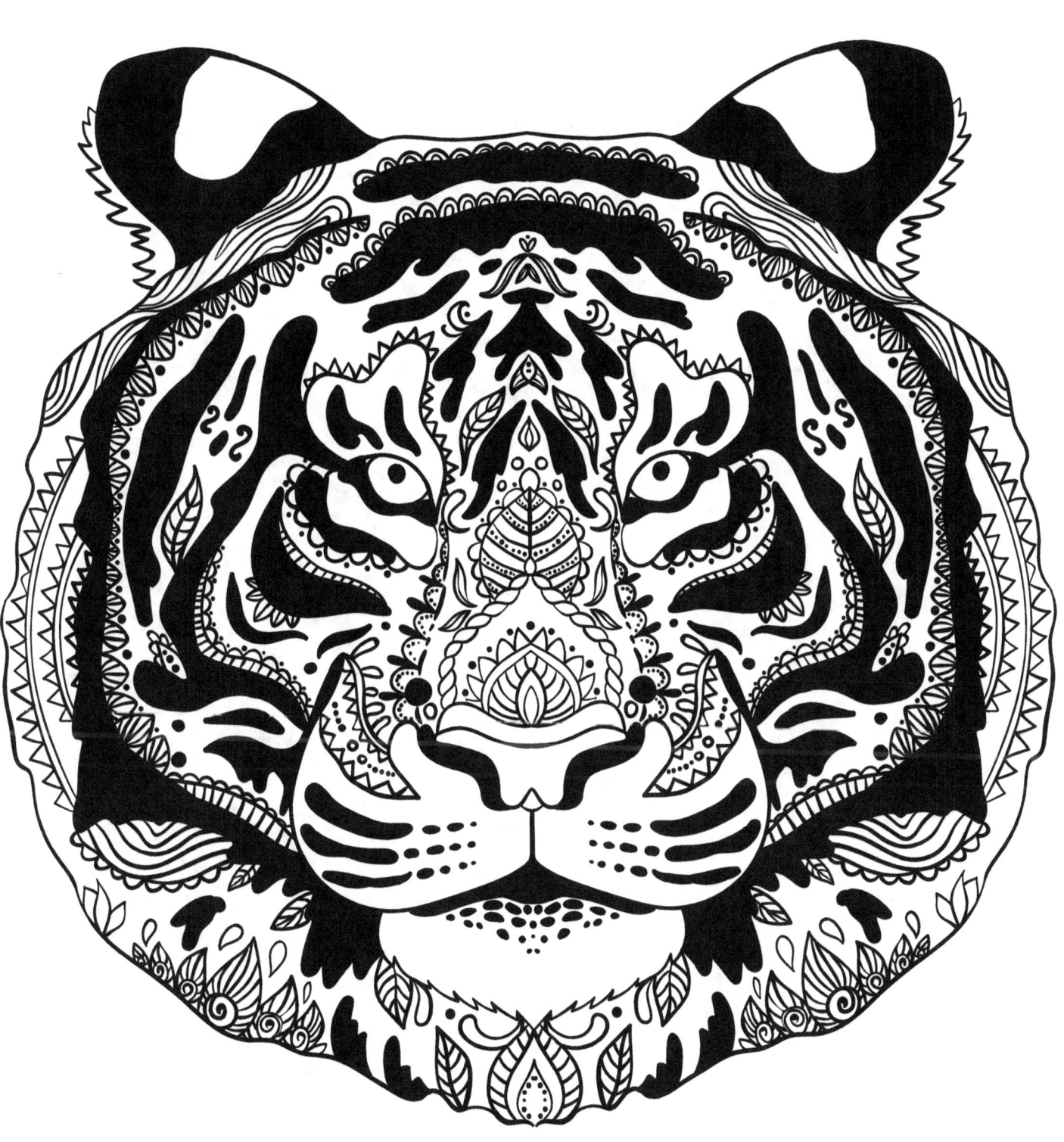

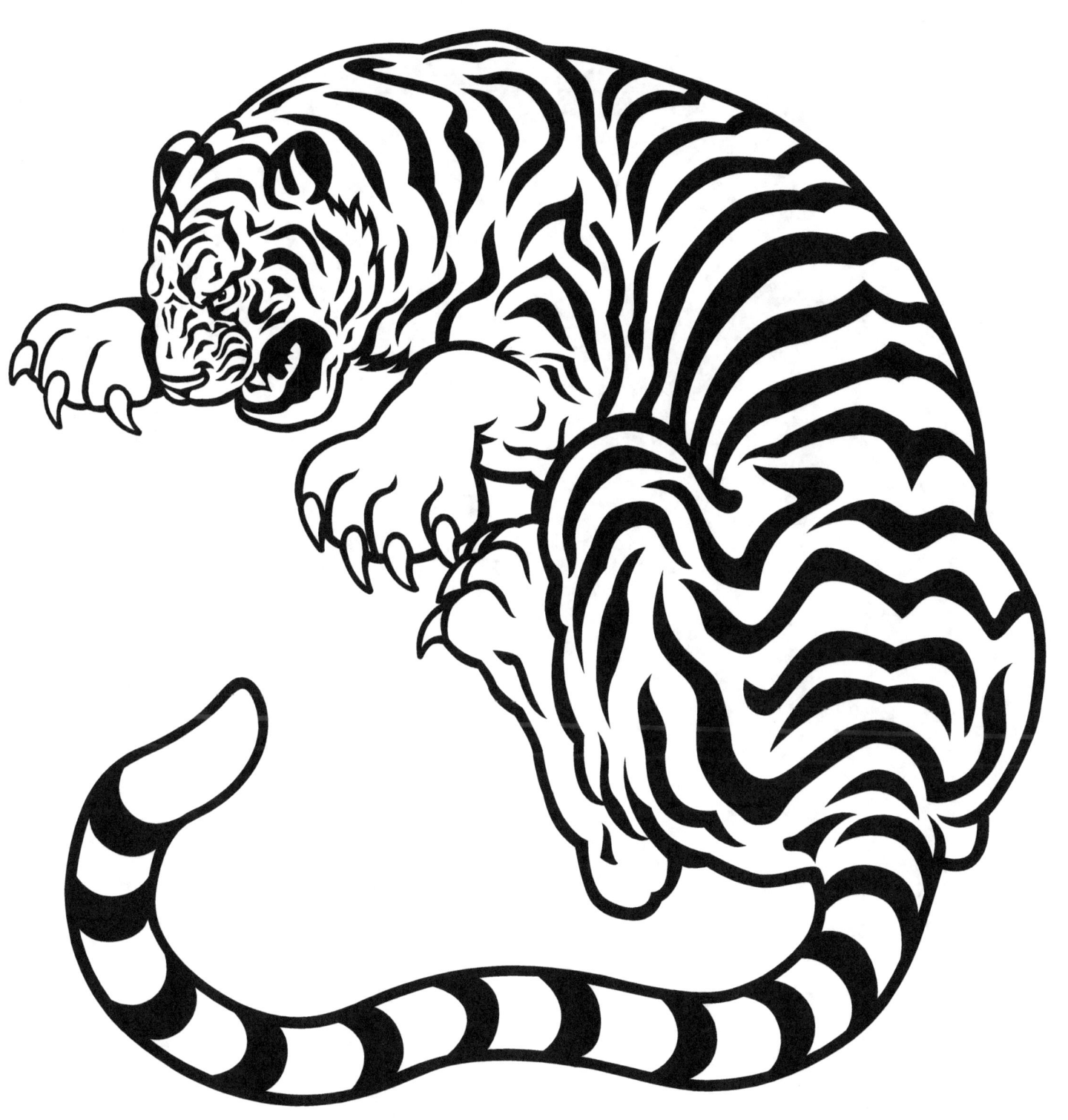

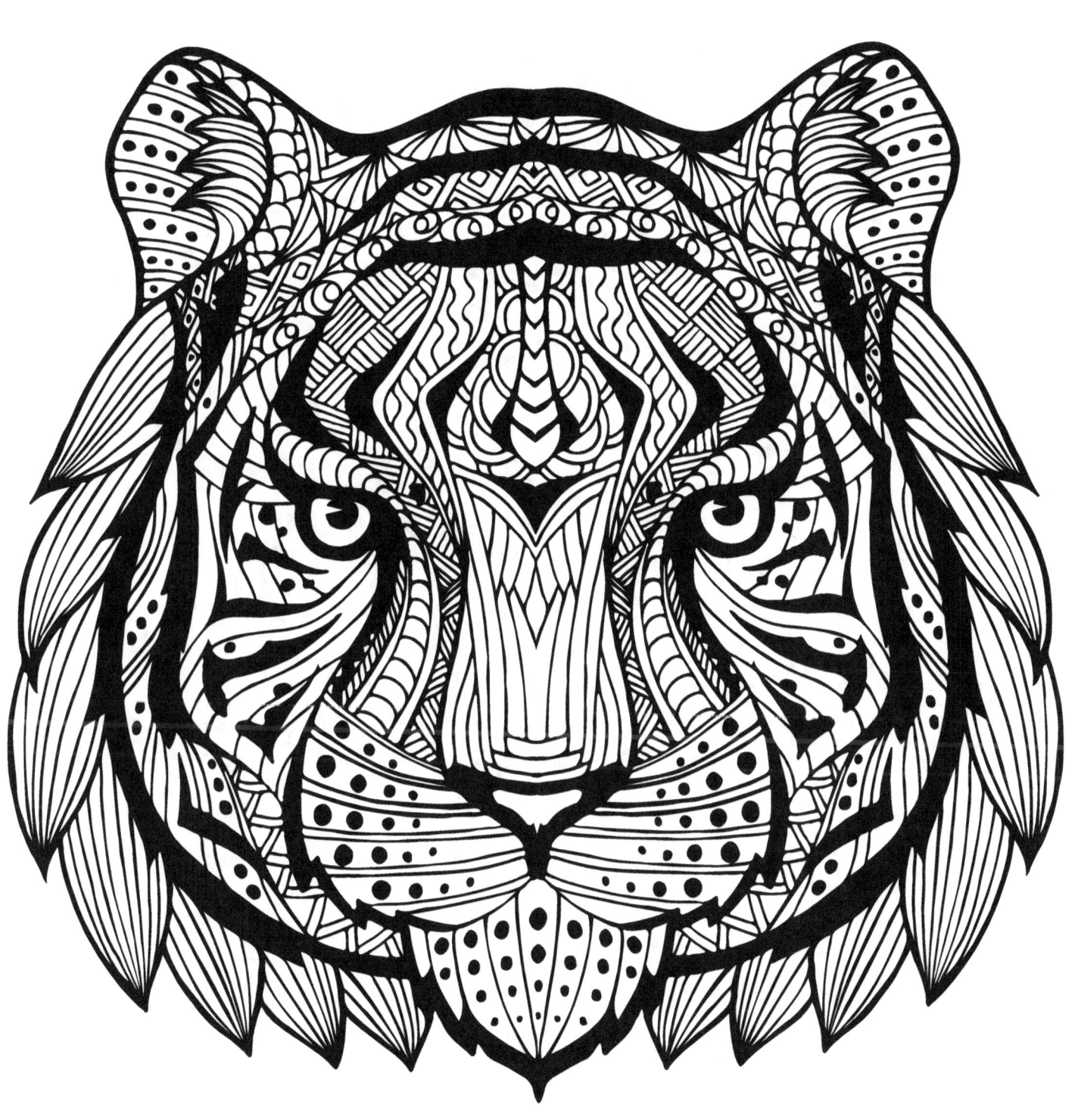

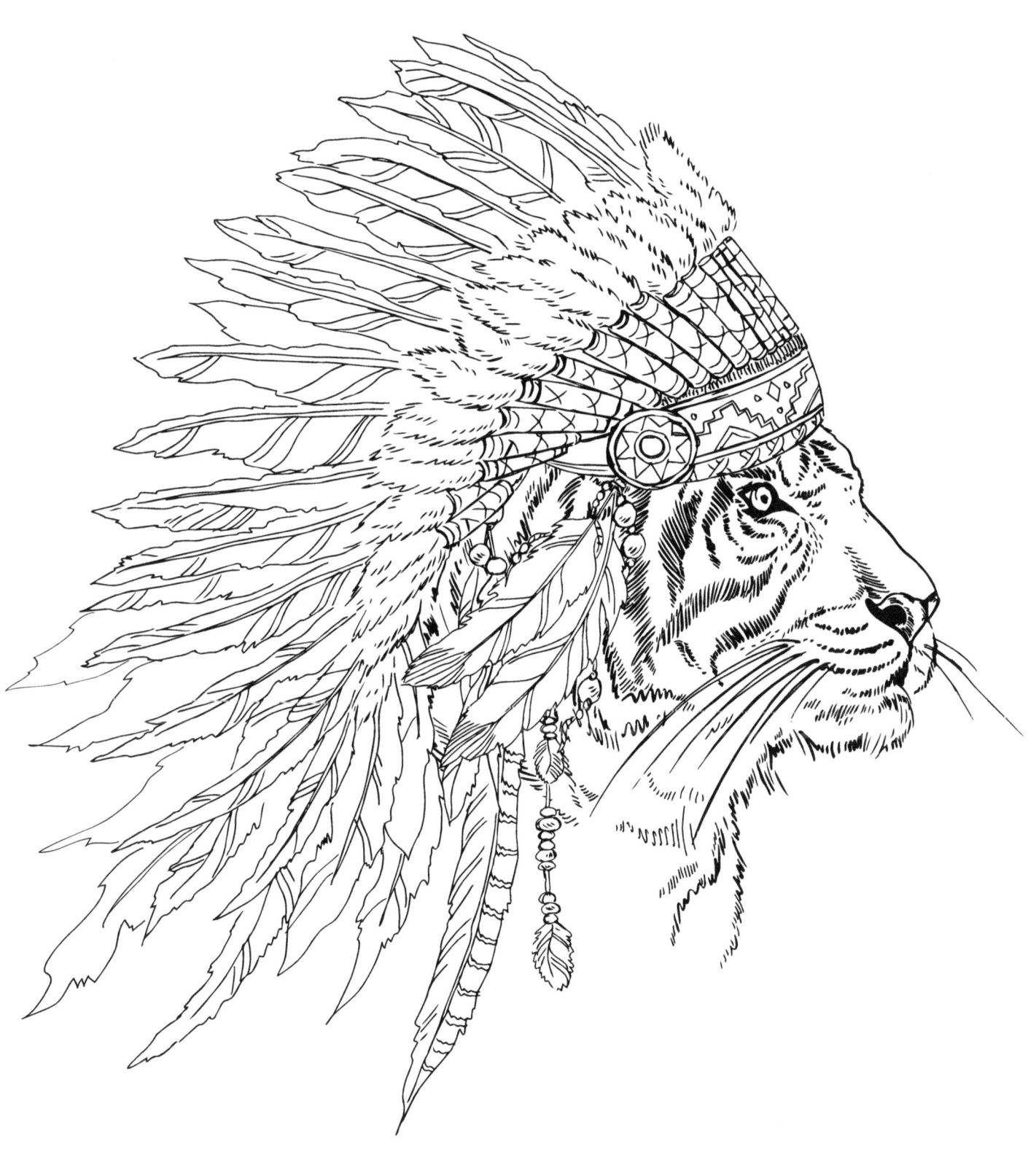

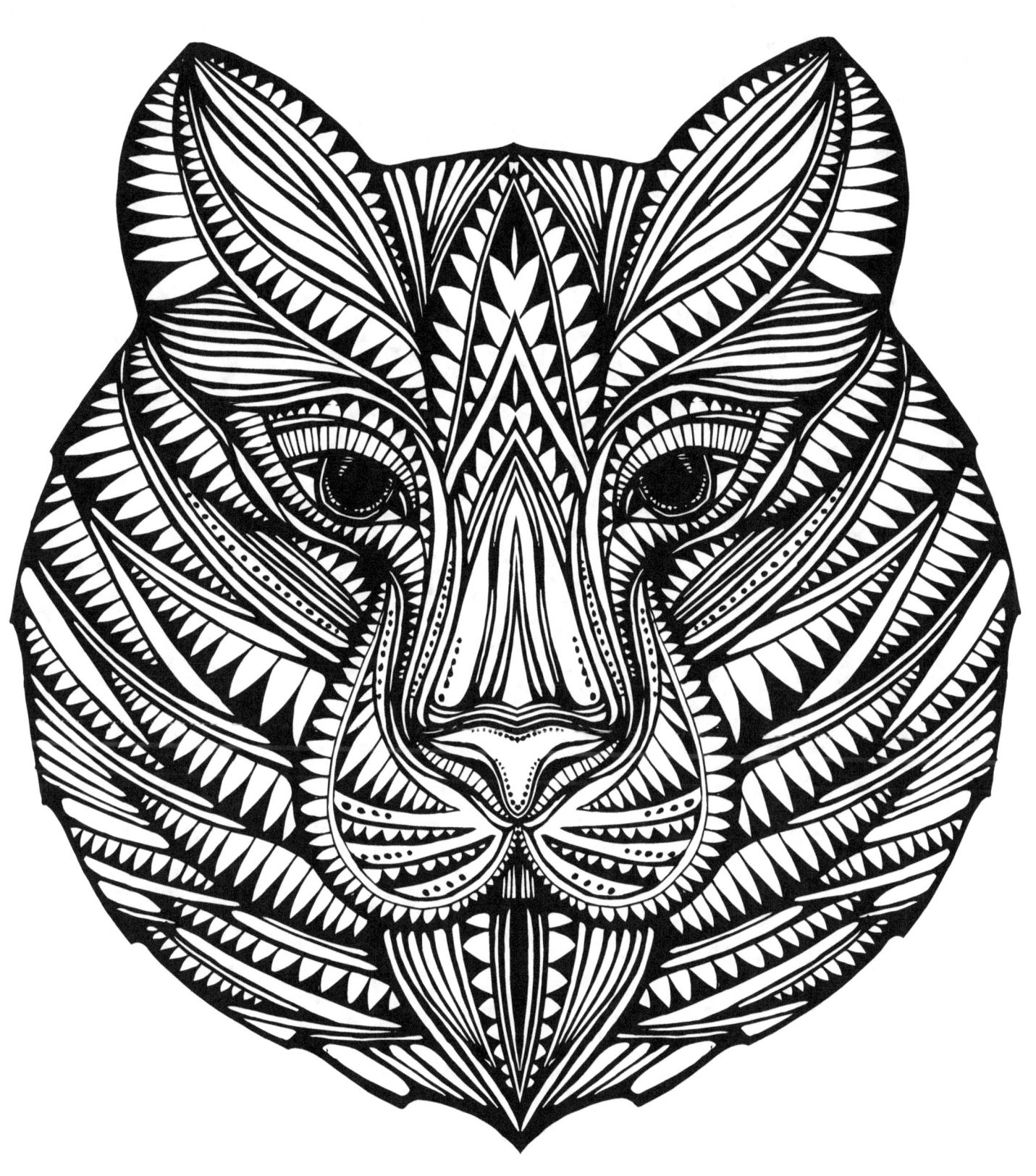

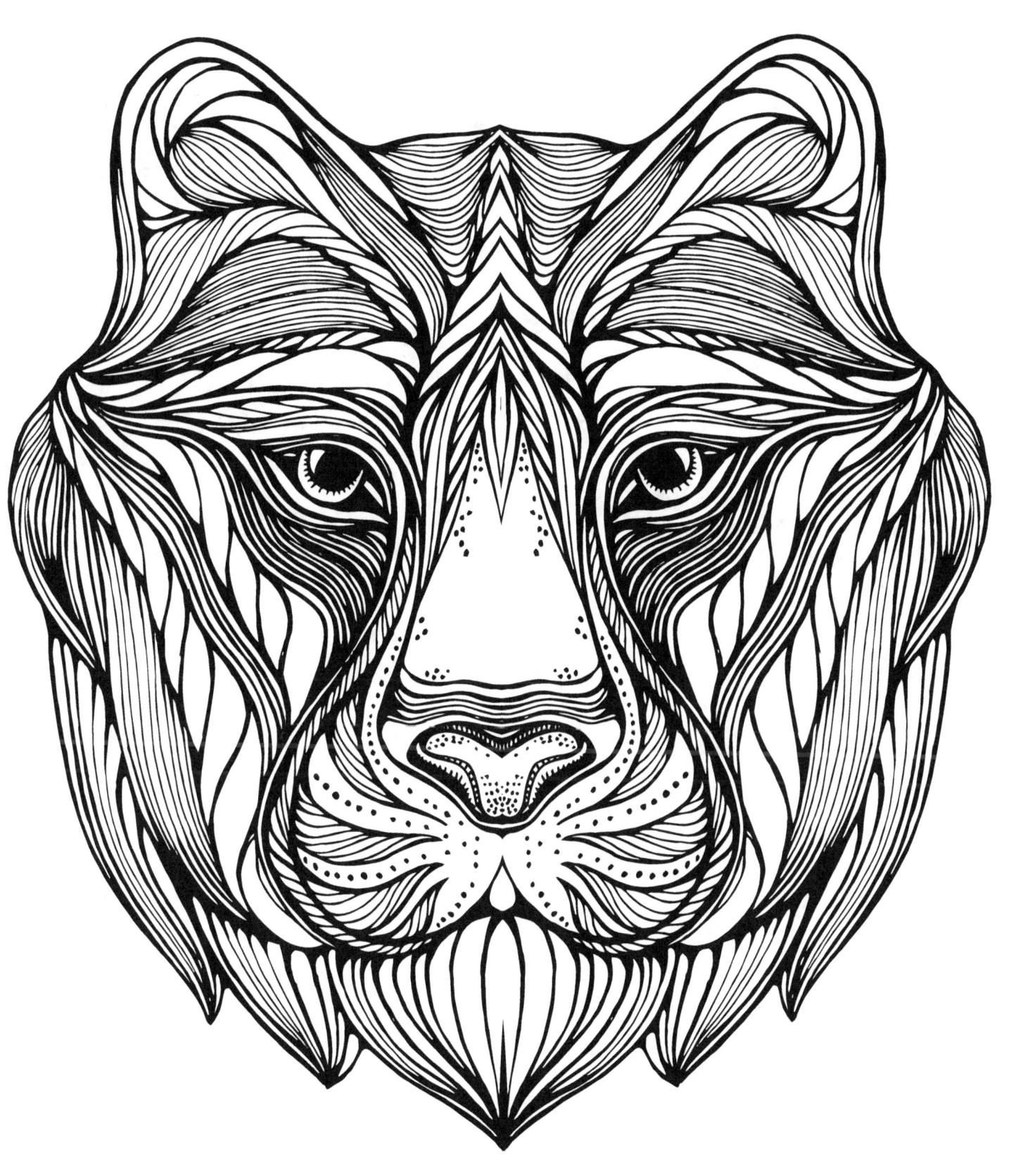

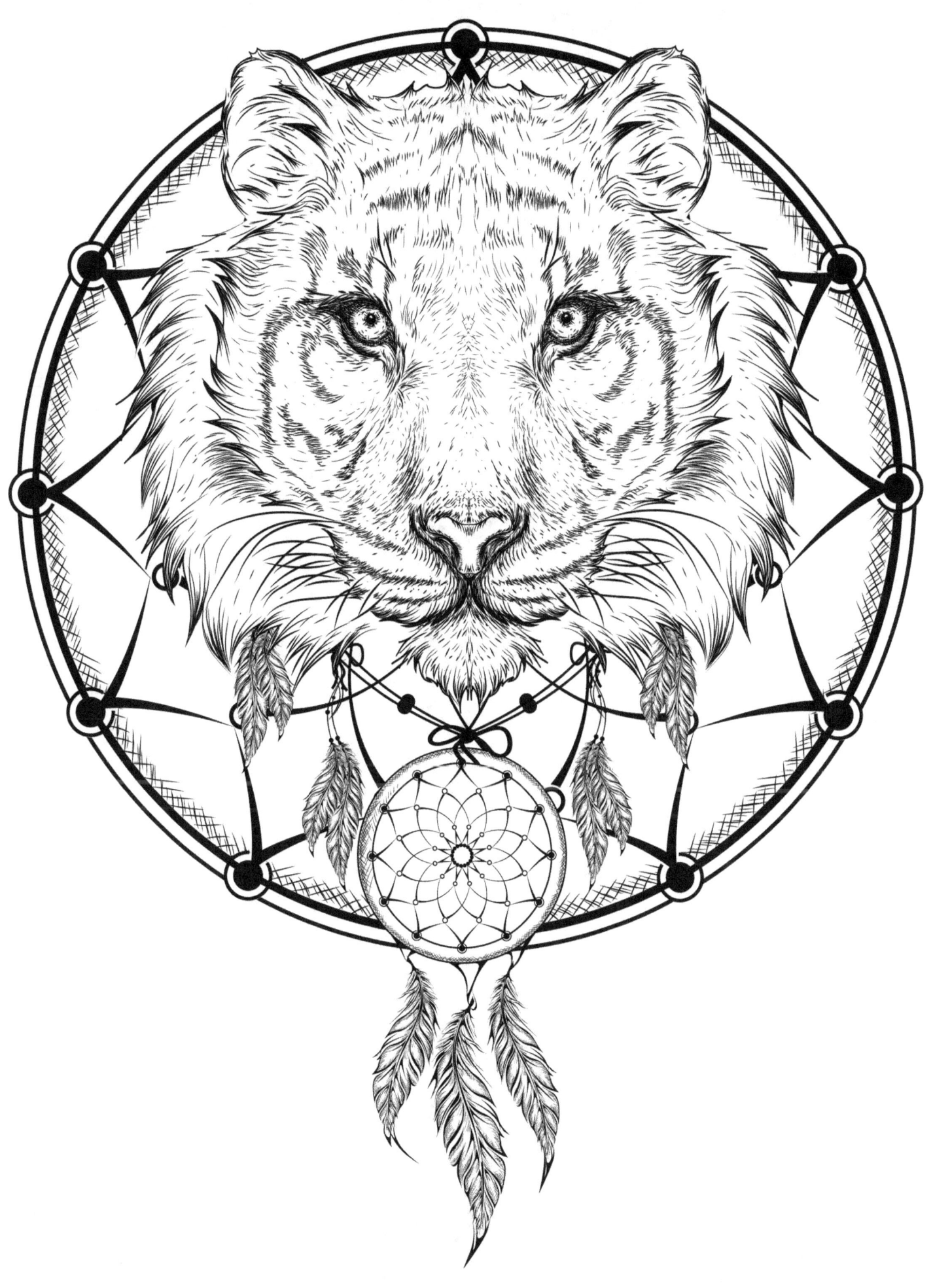

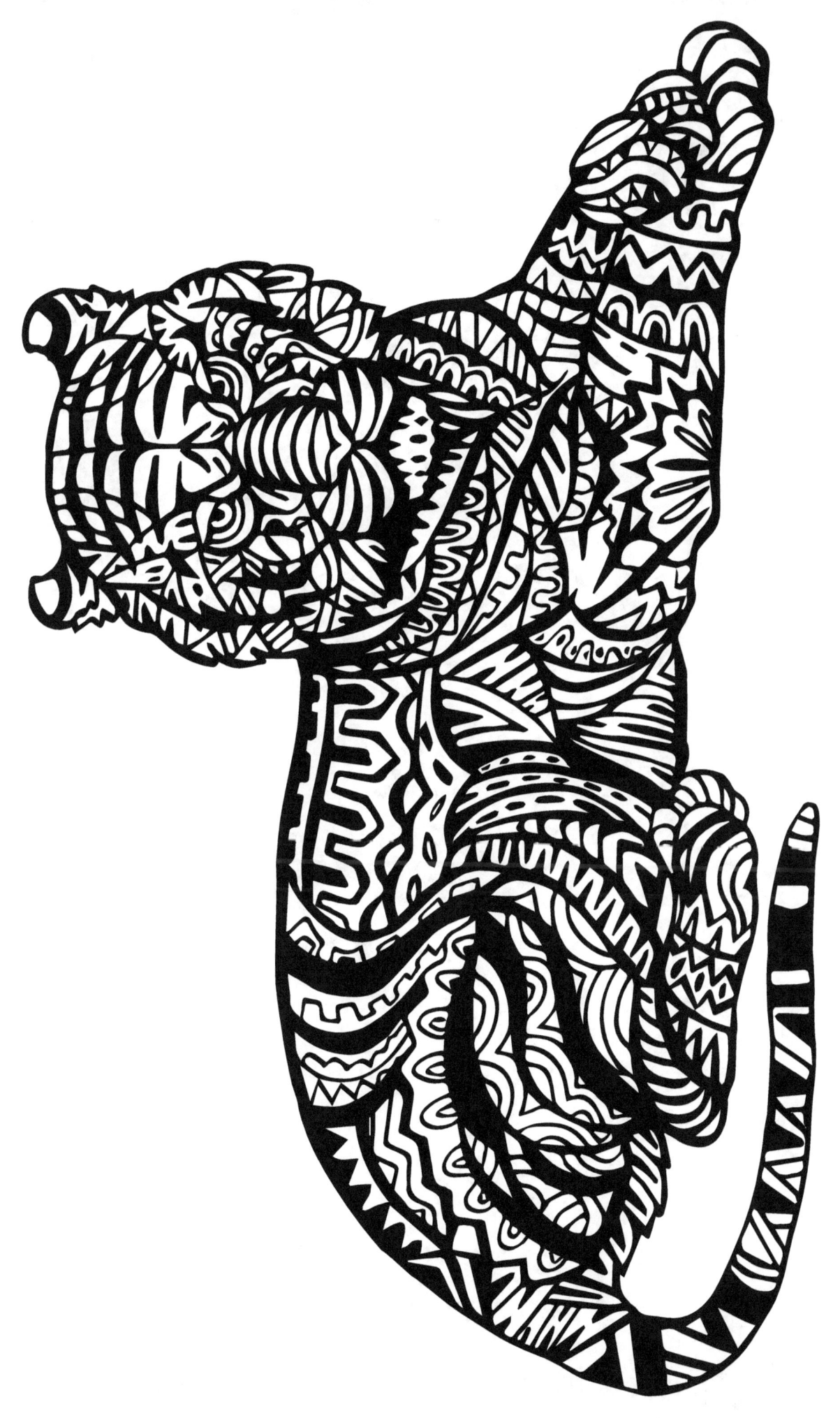

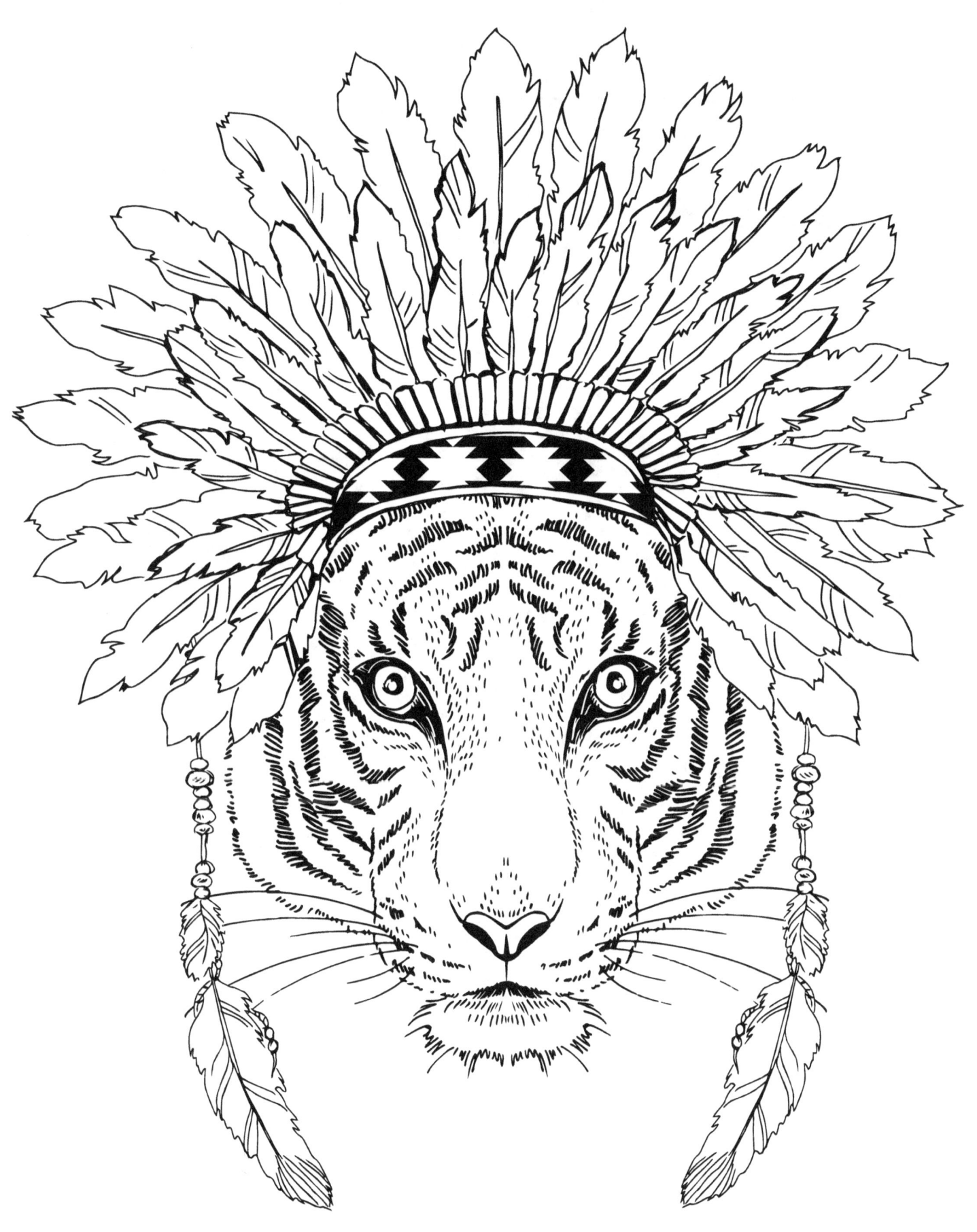

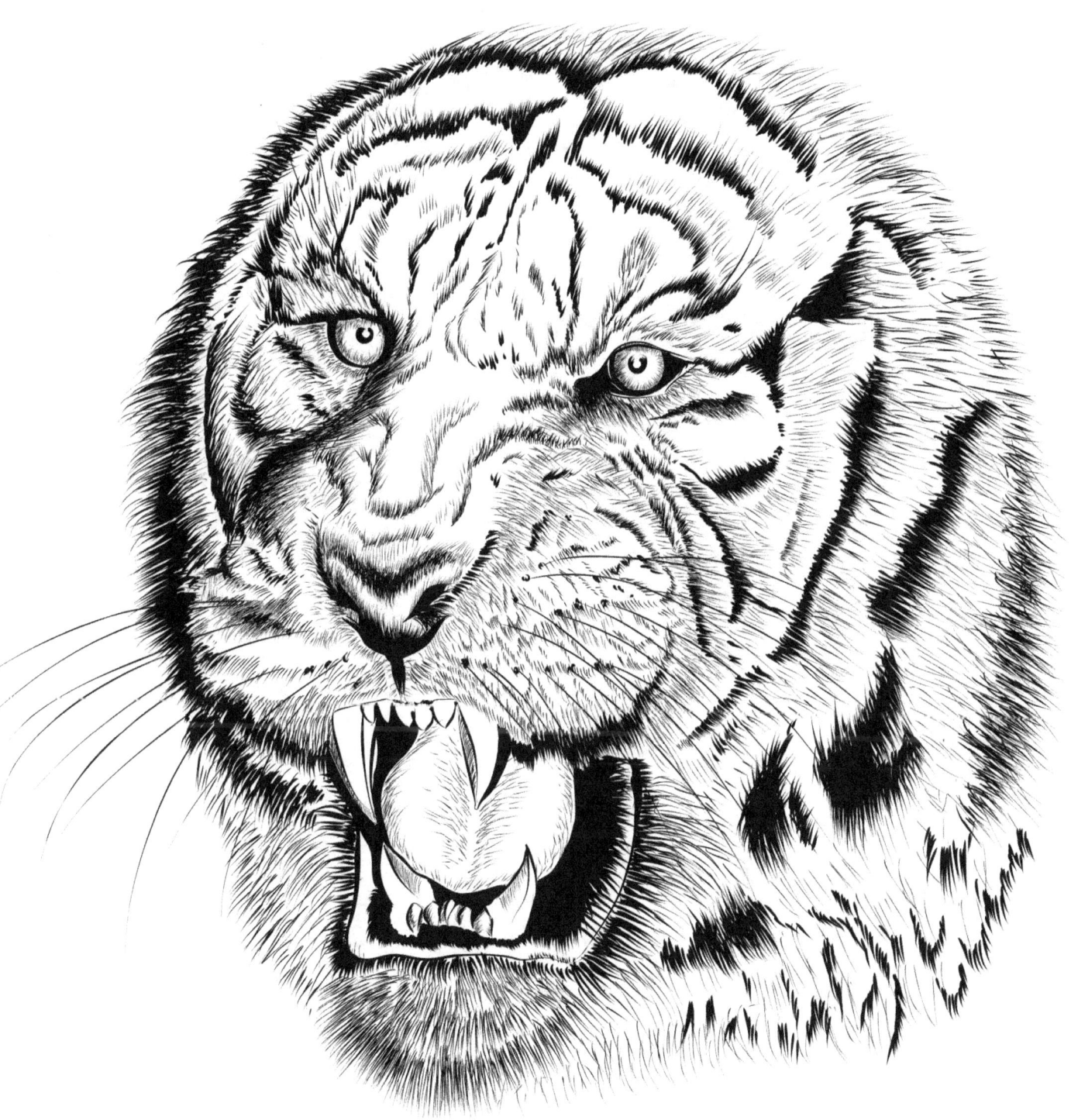

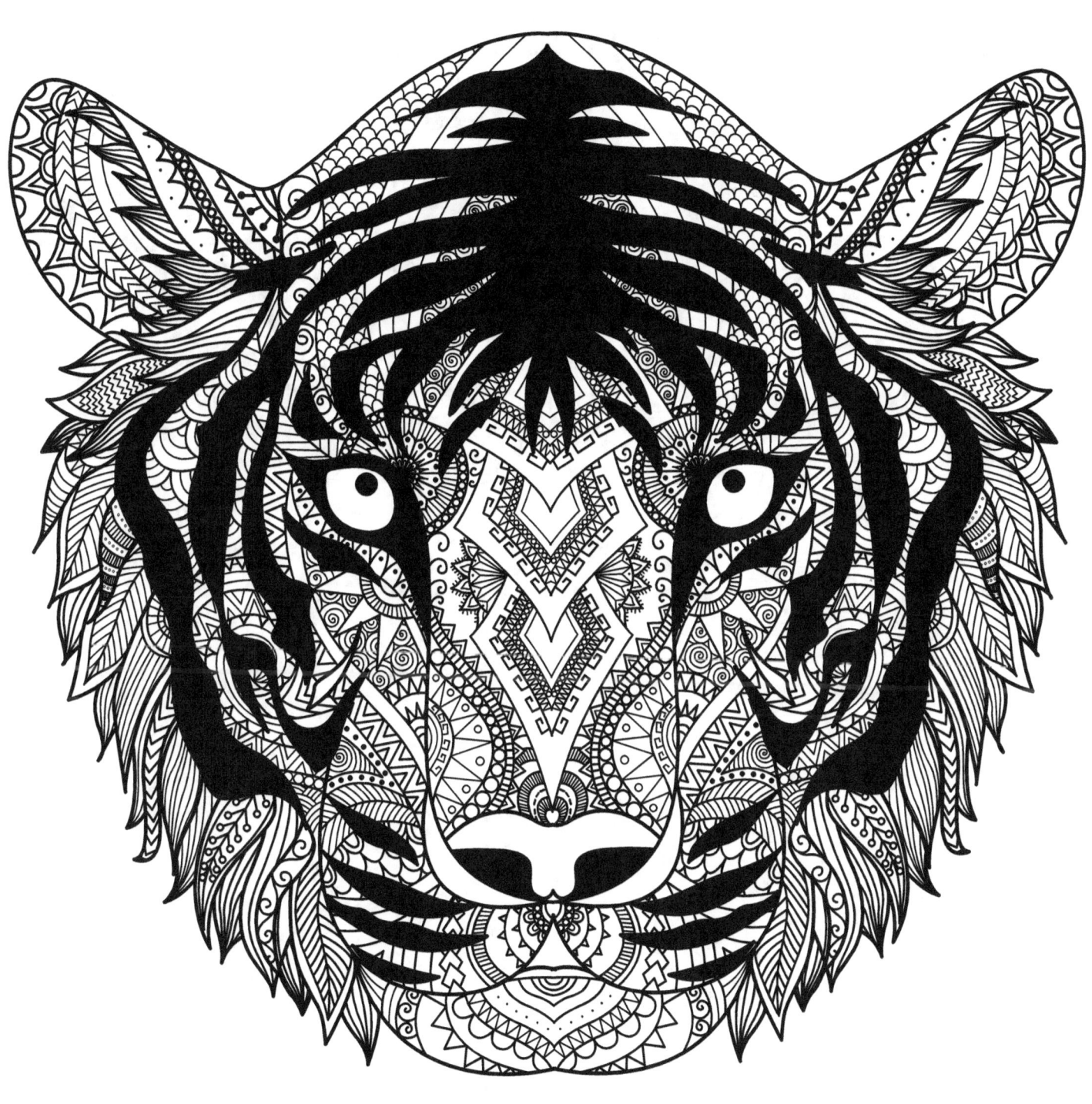

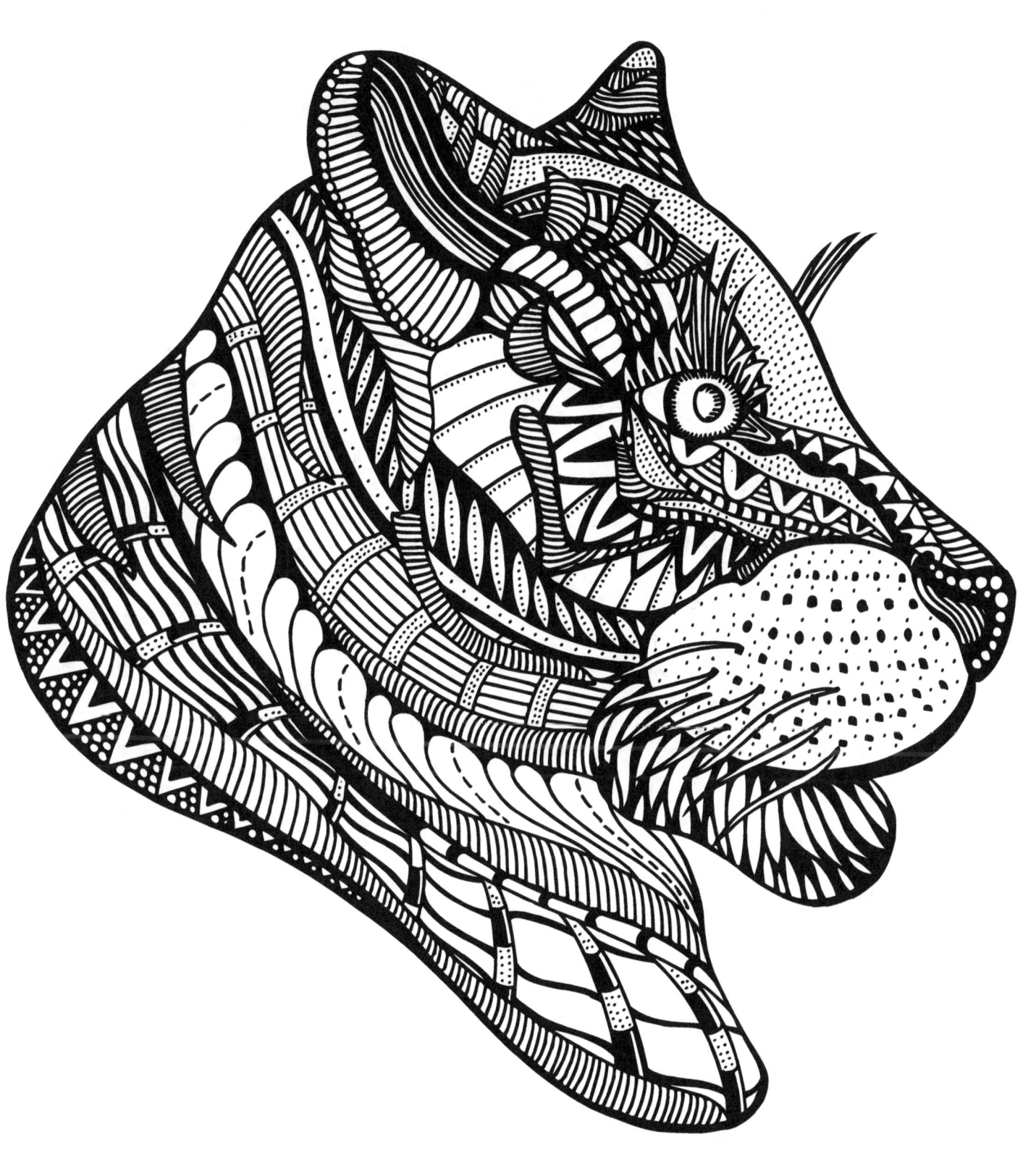

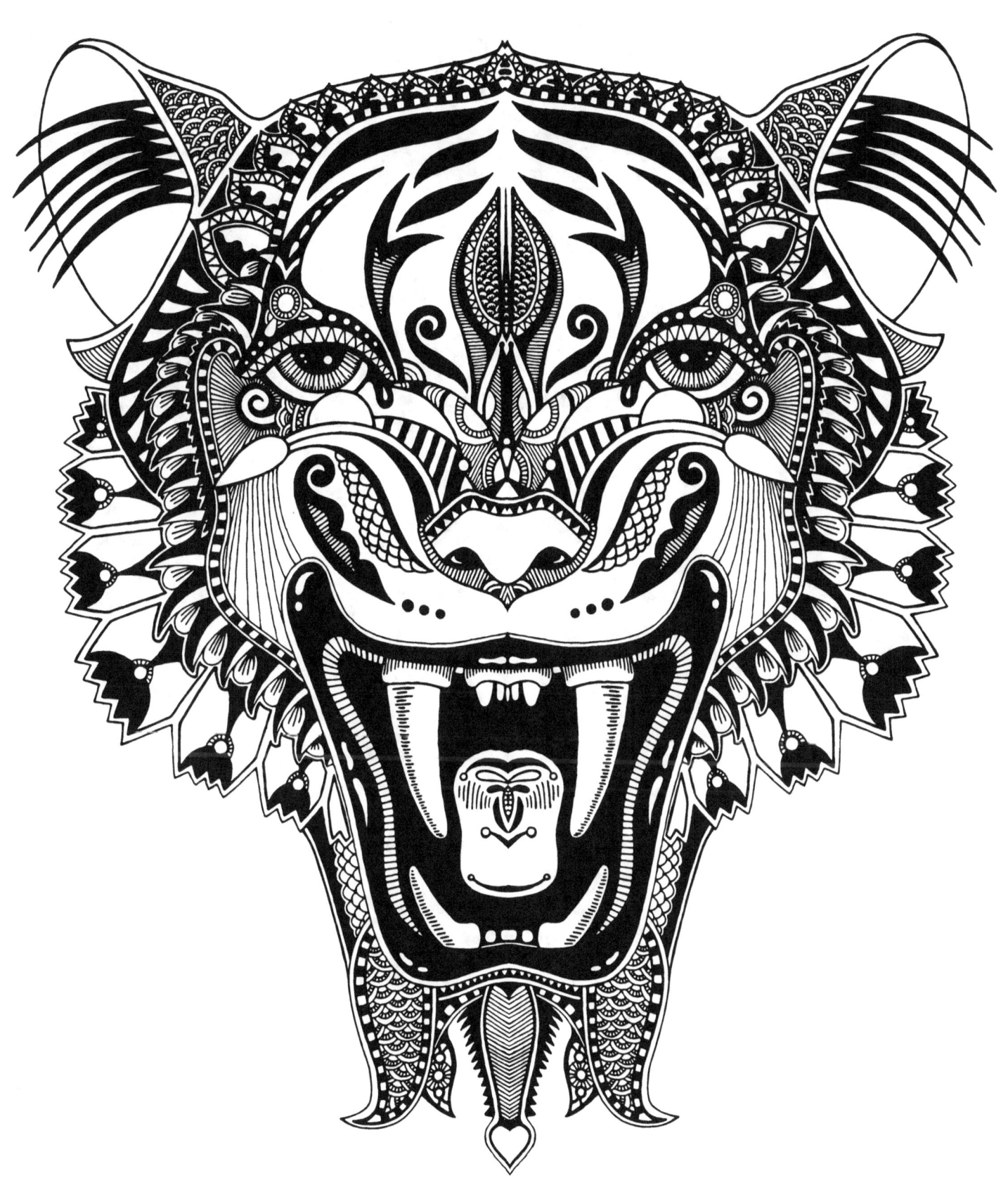

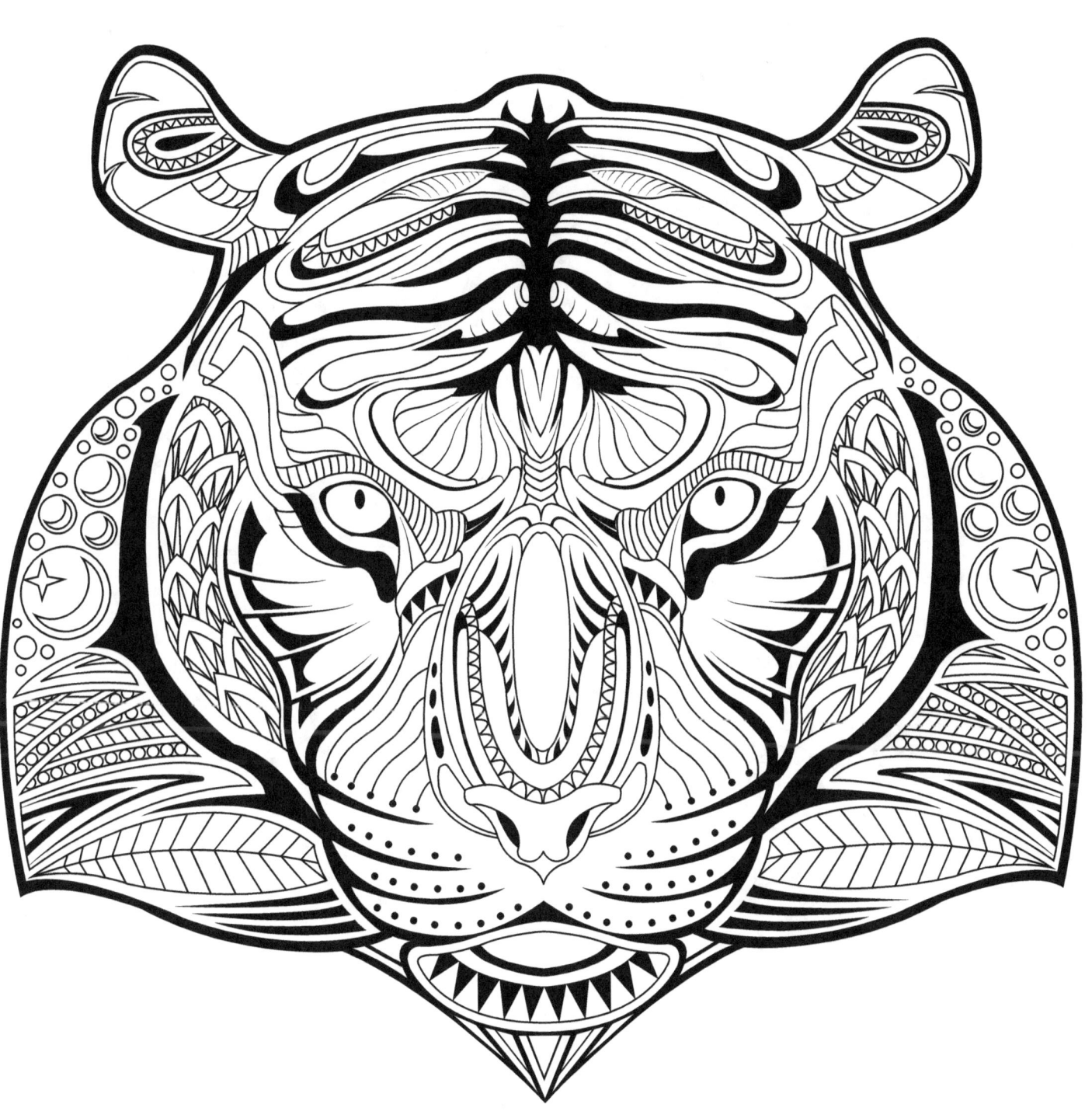

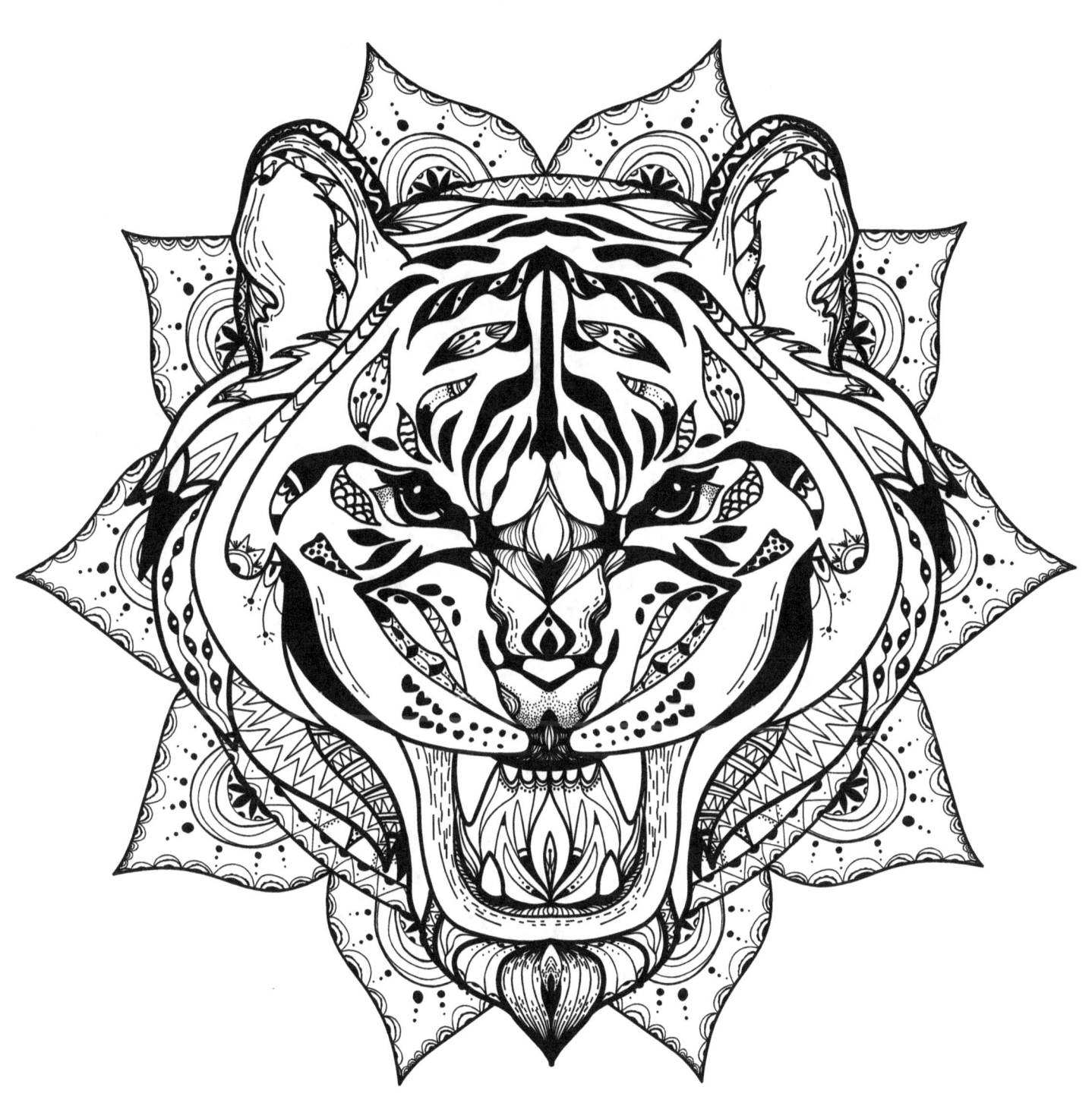

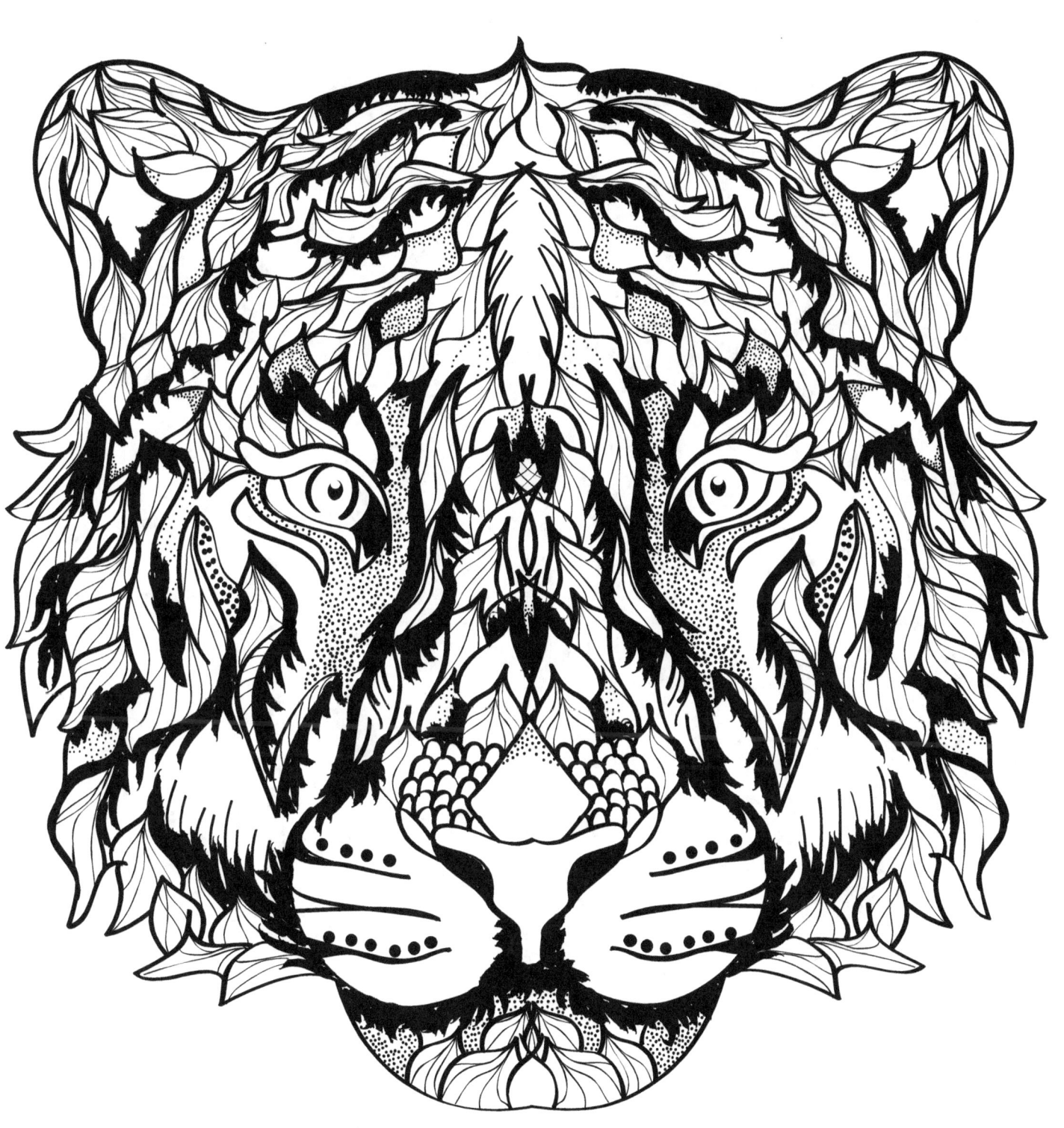

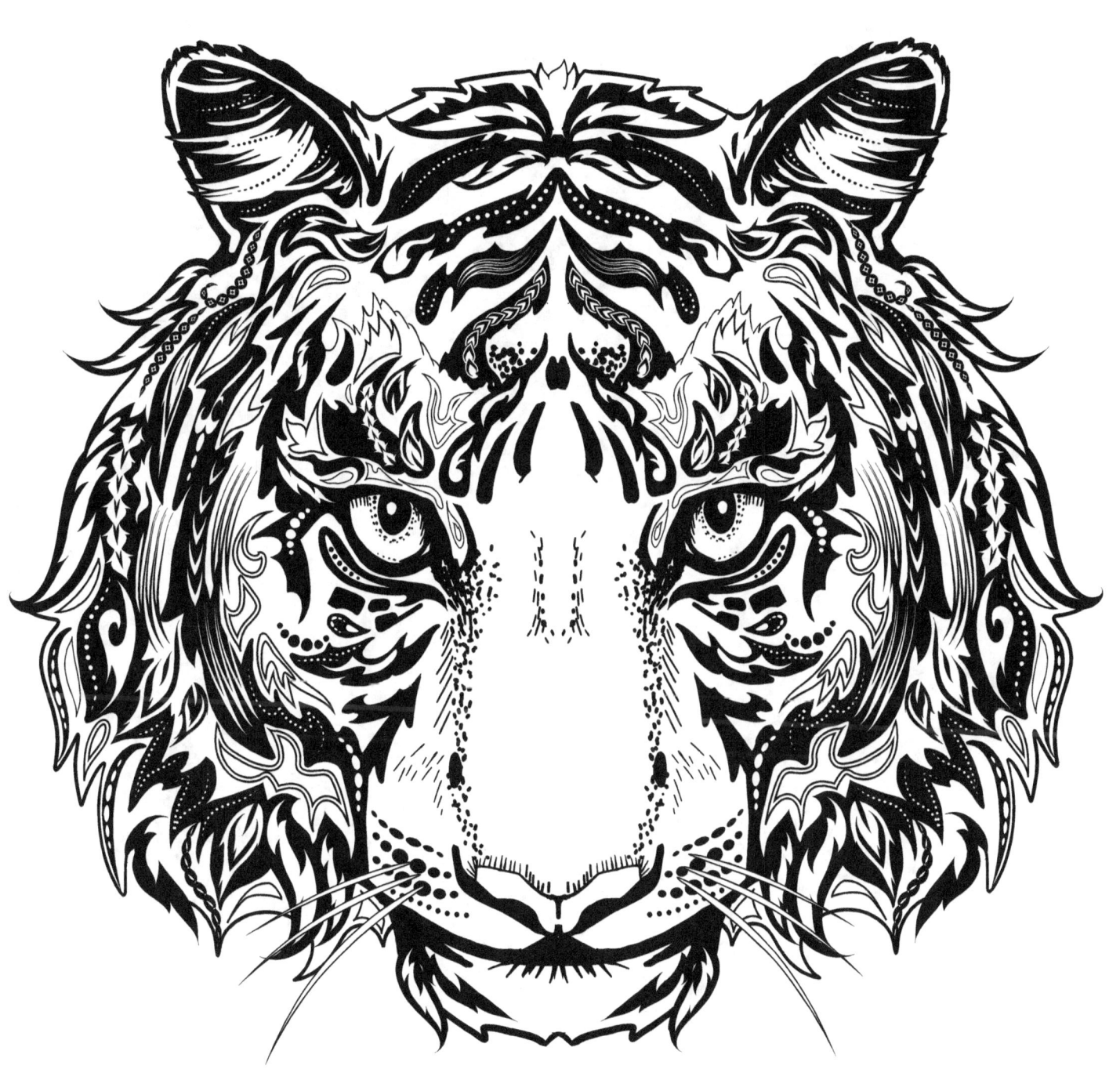

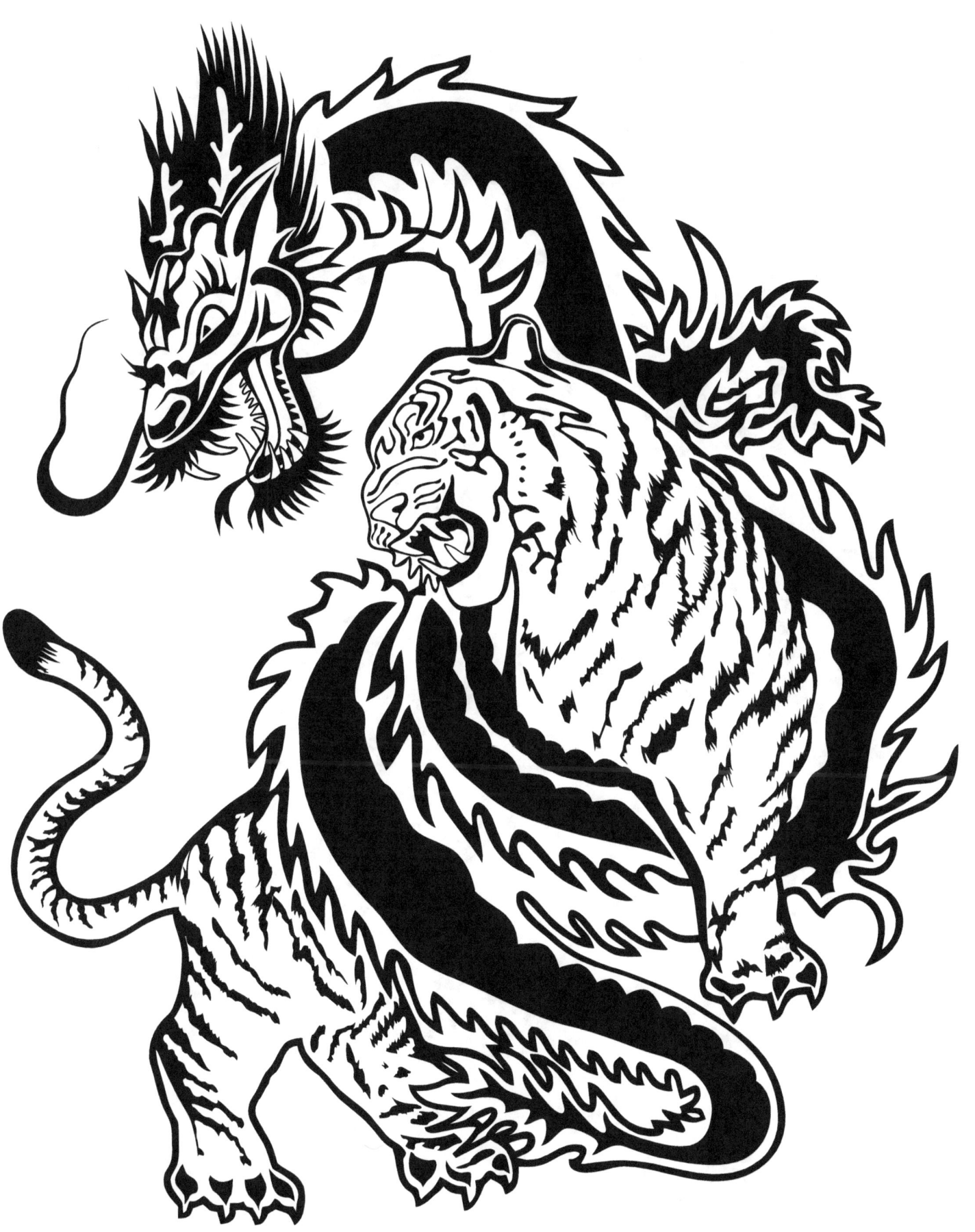

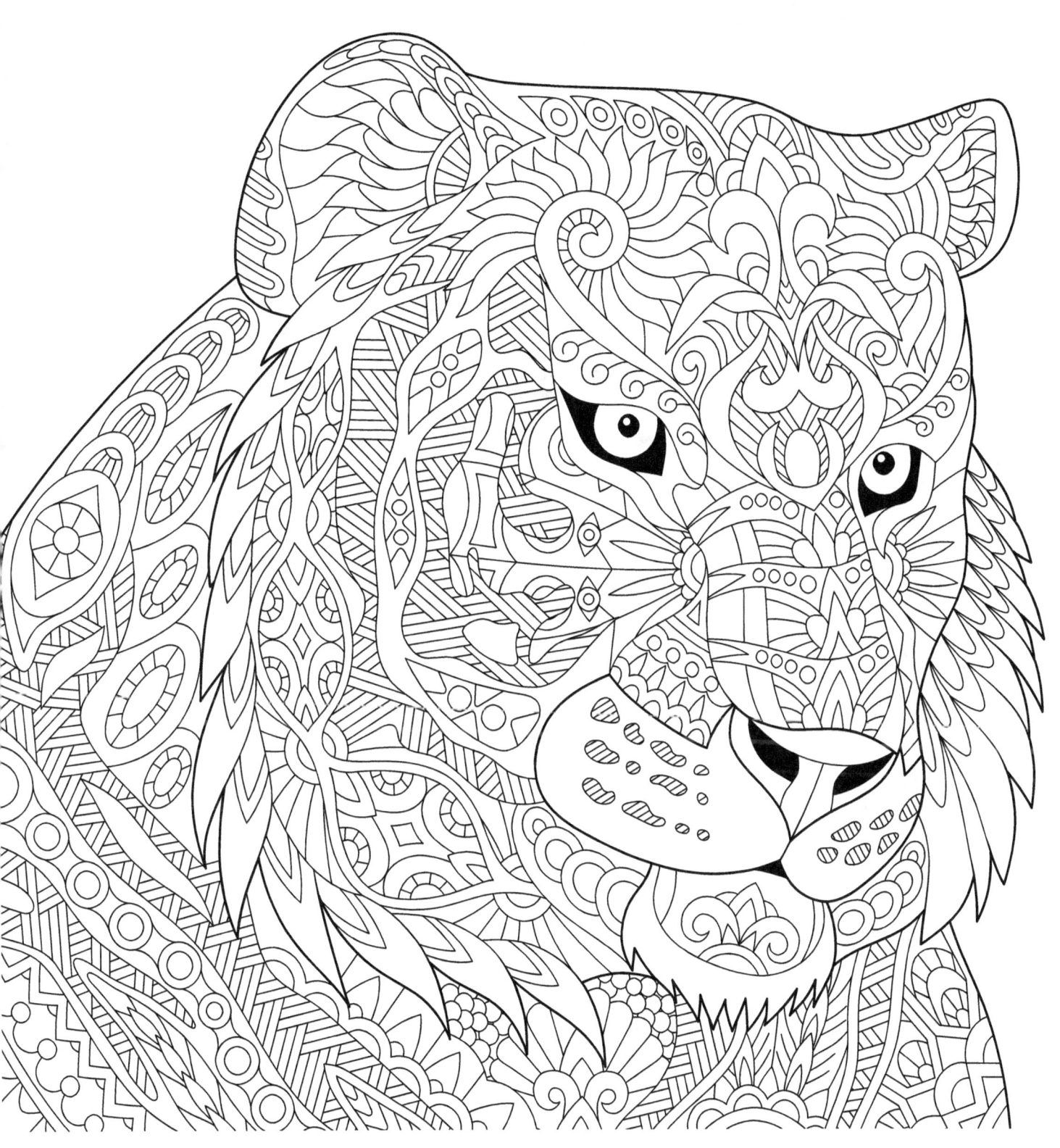

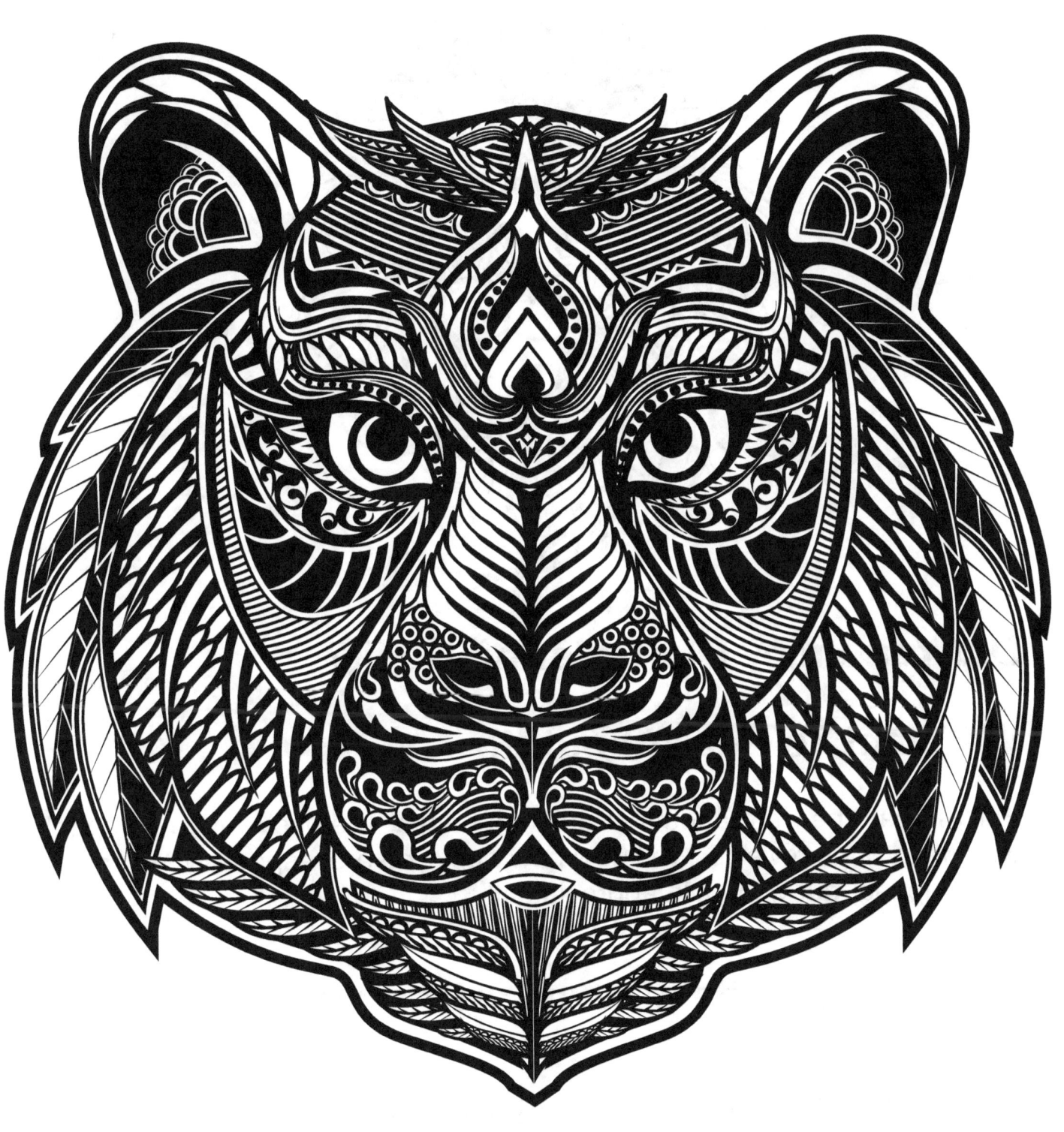

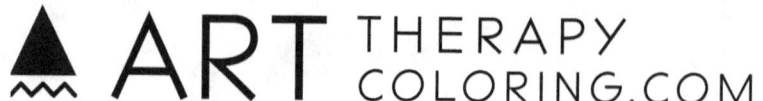

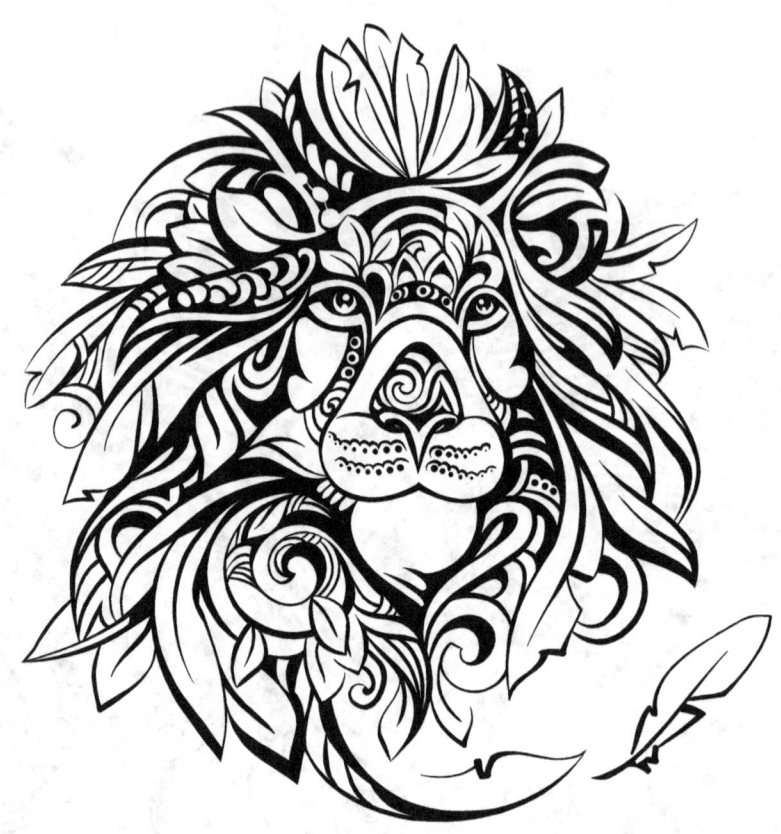

## Did You Enjoy Our Coloring Book?

## We Want To Hear About It!

Help spread the word about our coloring books! The best way to spread the word is through reviews. We know how busy you are, especially with all of that coloring, but we would appreciate it!

## Visit our website at www.arttherapycoloring.com

## Over 200 Art Therapy Coloring Books

See our collection of over 200 Art Therapy Coloring Books for Adults, Men, Women, Seniors, Teens, Kids, Boys, and Girls.

# Coloring Books For Adults

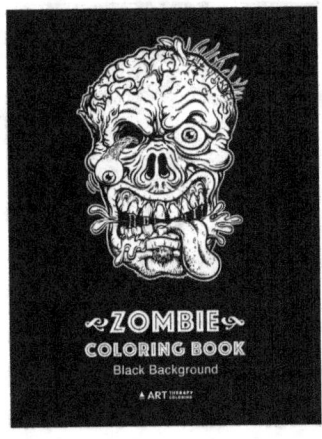

**ZOMBIE**
COLORING BOOK
Black Background

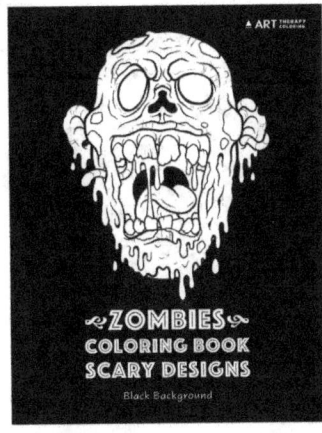

**ZOMBIES**
COLORING BOOK
SCARY DESIGNS
Black Background

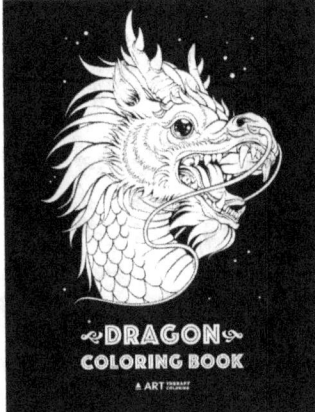

**DRAGON**
COLORING BOOK

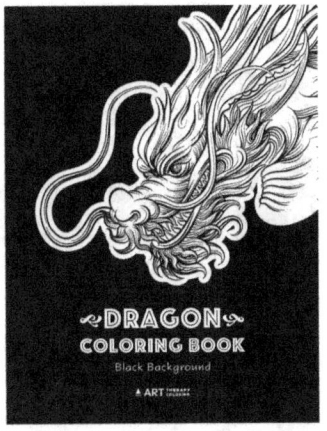

**DRAGON**
COLORING BOOK
Black Background

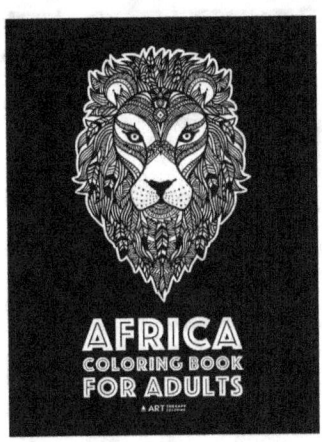

**AFRICA**
COLORING BOOK
FOR ADULTS

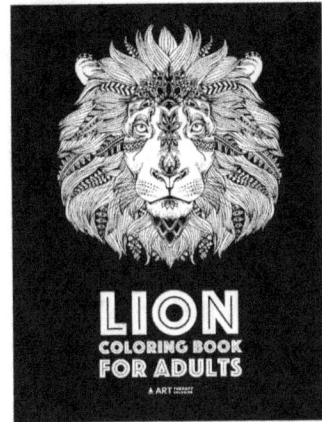

**LION**
COLORING BOOK
FOR ADULTS

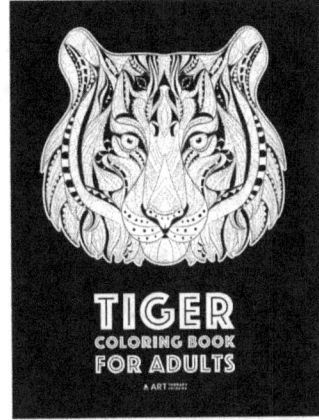

**TIGER**
COLORING BOOK
FOR ADULTS

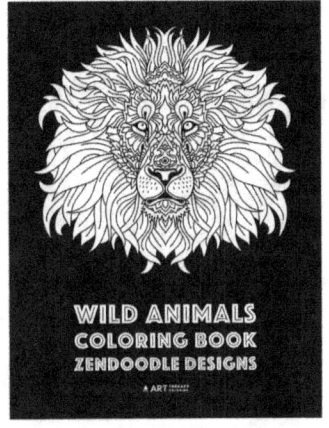

**WILD ANIMALS**
COLORING BOOK
ZENDOODLE DESIGNS

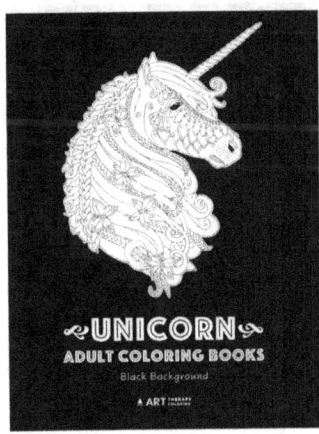

**UNICORN**
ADULT COLORING BOOKS
Black Background

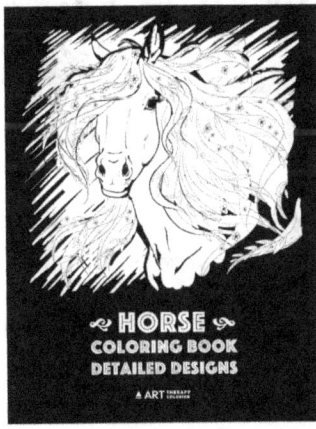

**HORSE**
COLORING BOOK
DETAILED DESIGNS

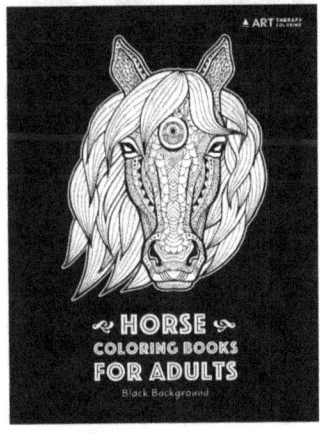

**HORSE**
COLORING BOOKS
FOR ADULTS
Black Background

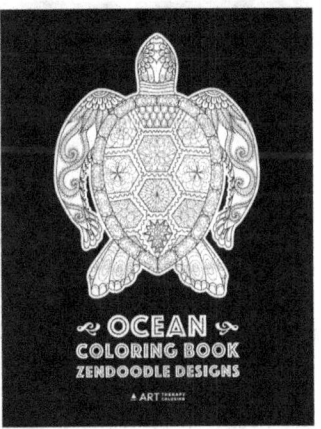

**OCEAN**
COLORING BOOK
ZENDOODLE DESIGNS

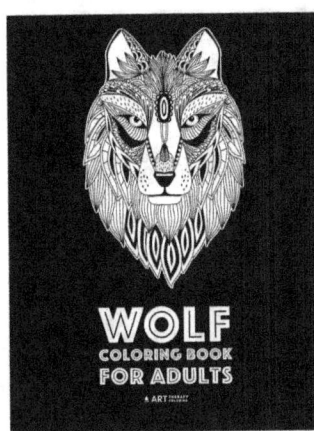

**WOLF**
COLORING BOOK
FOR ADULTS

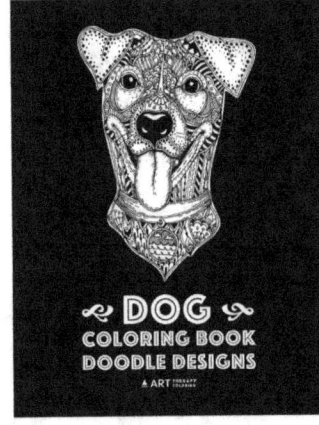

**DOG**
COLORING BOOK
DOODLE DESIGNS

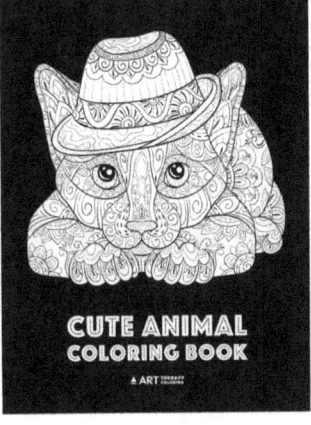

**CUTE ANIMAL**
COLORING BOOK

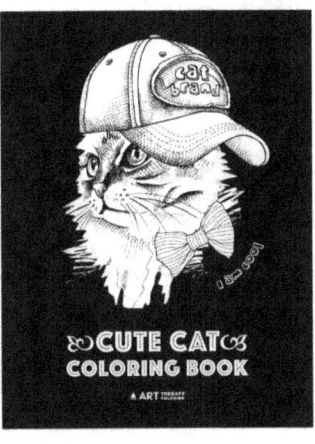

**CUTE CAT**
COLORING BOOK

# Coloring Books For Adults

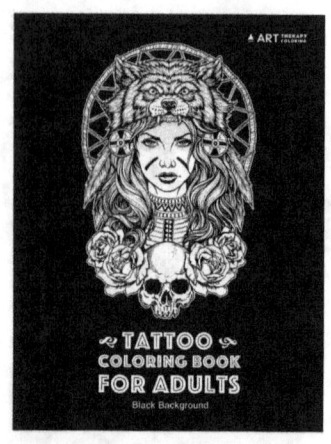

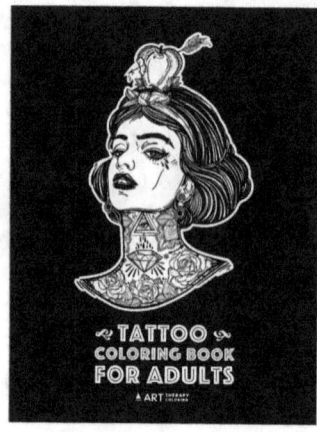

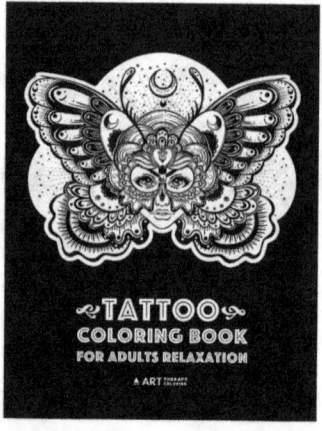

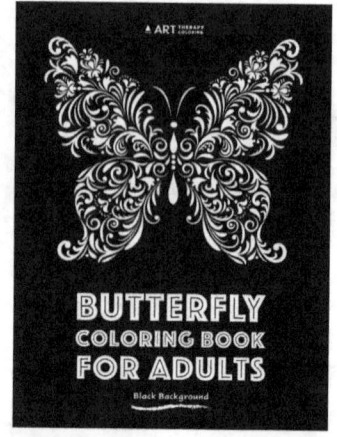

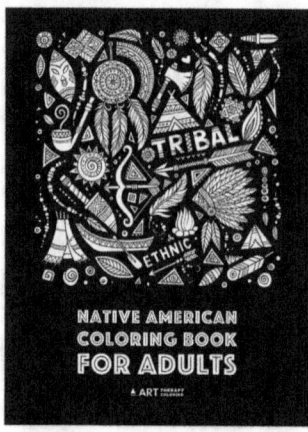

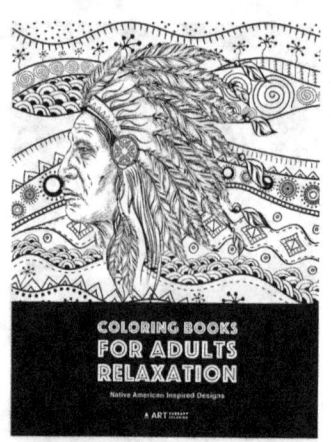

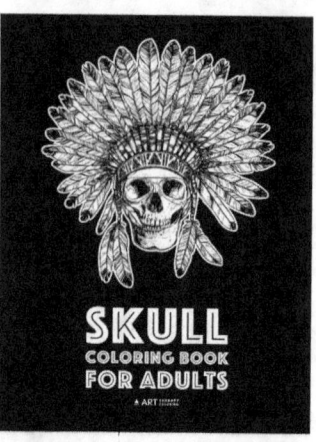

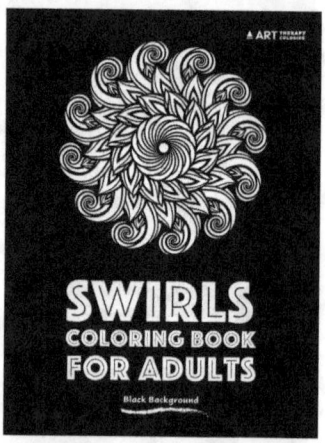

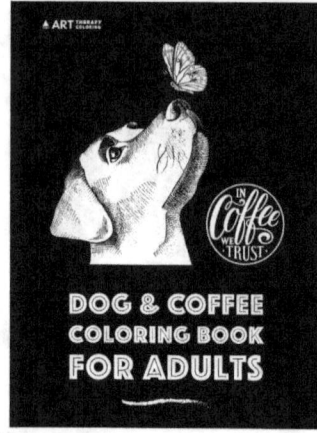

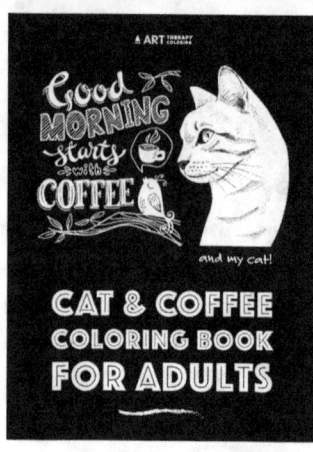

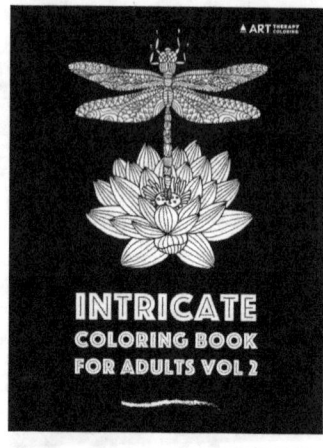

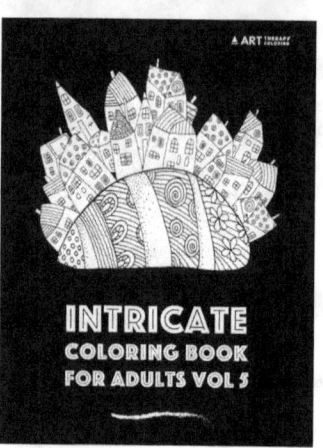

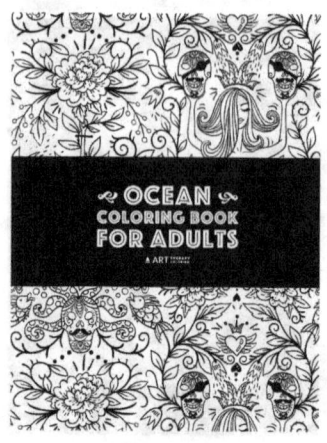

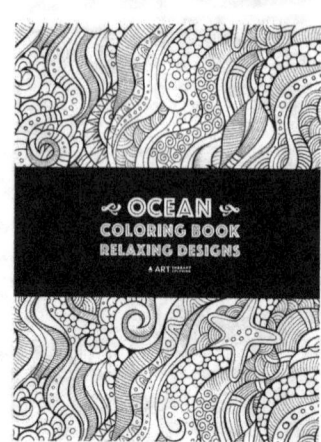

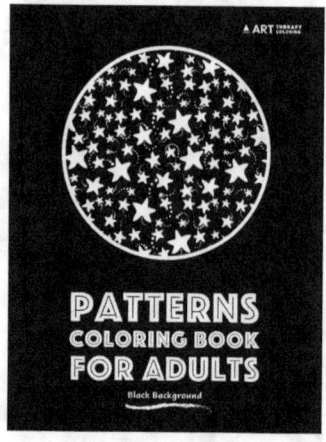

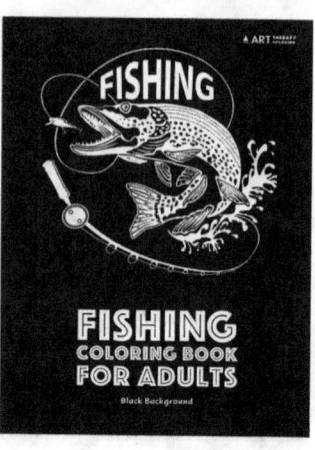

# Coloring Books For Adults

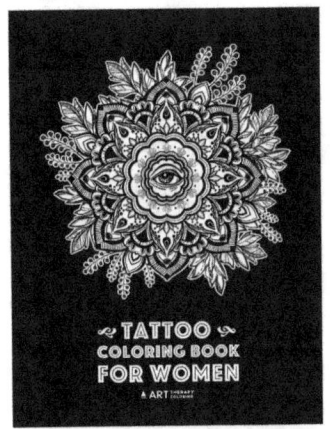

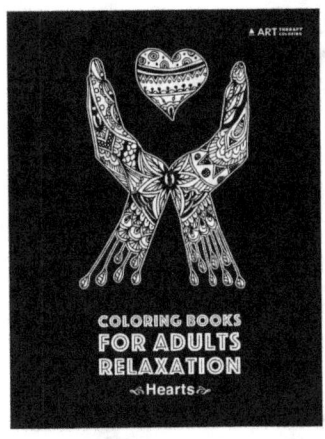

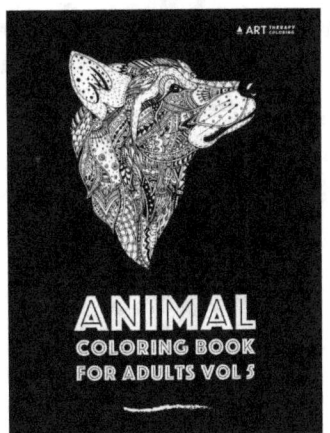

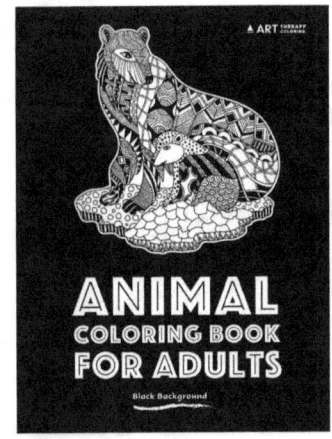

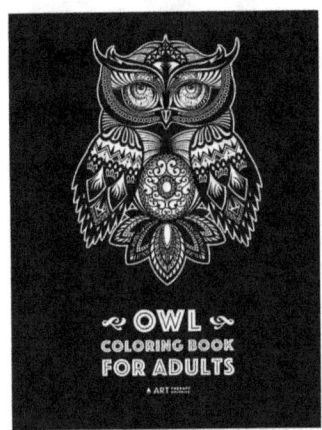

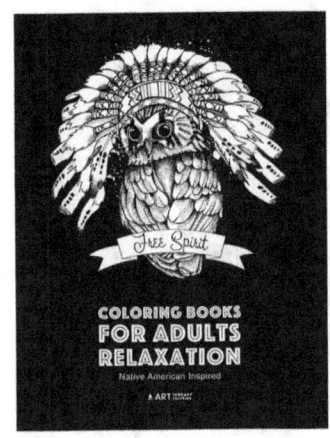

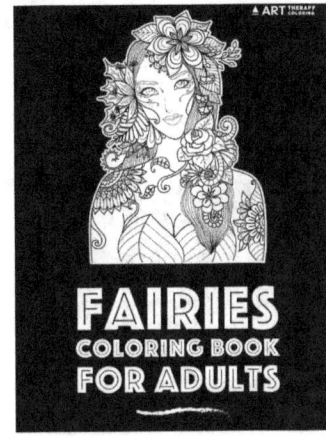

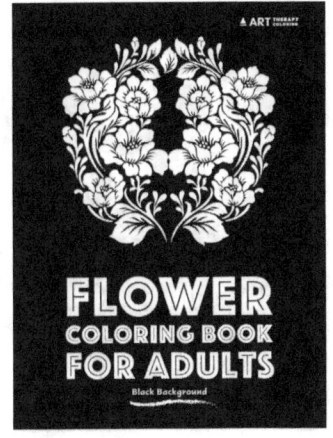

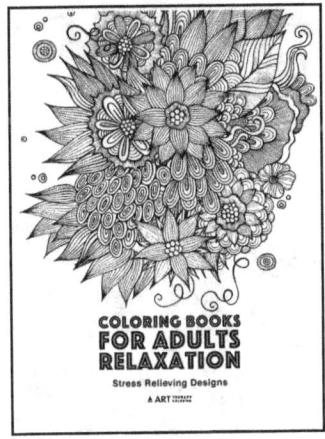

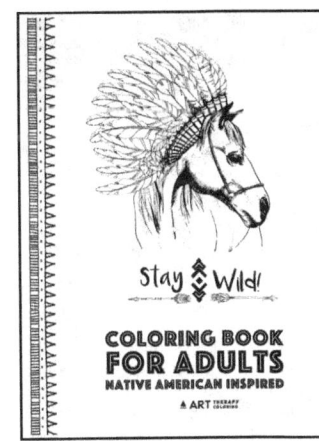

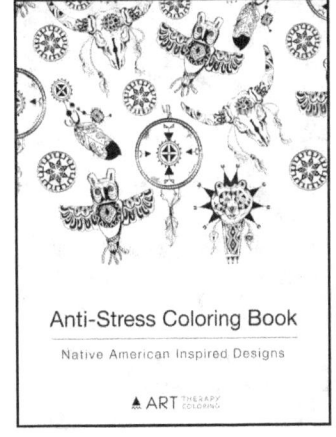

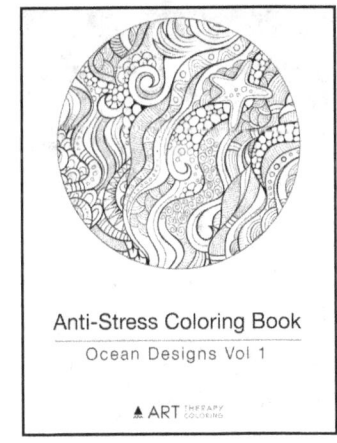

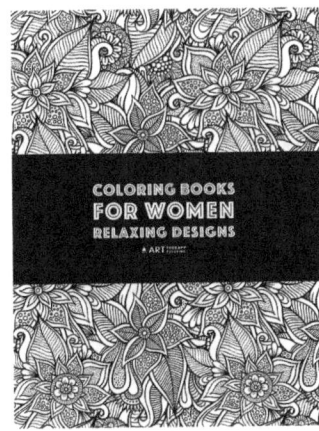

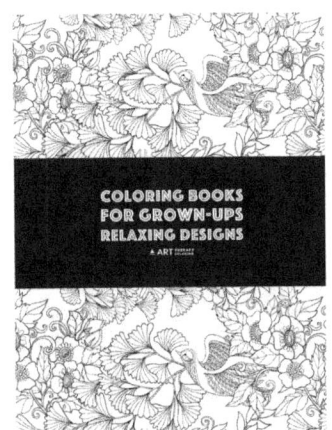

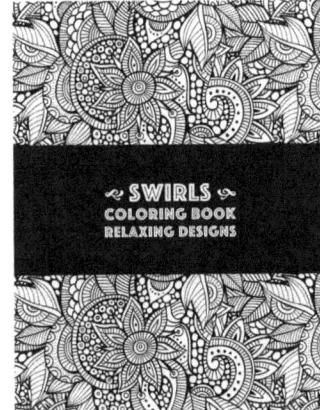

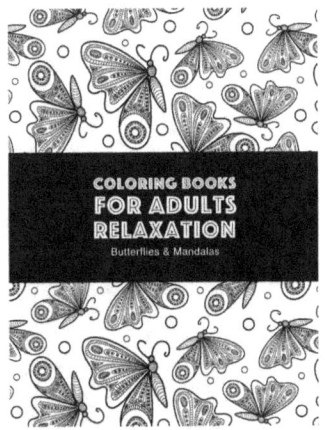

# Coloring Books For Men

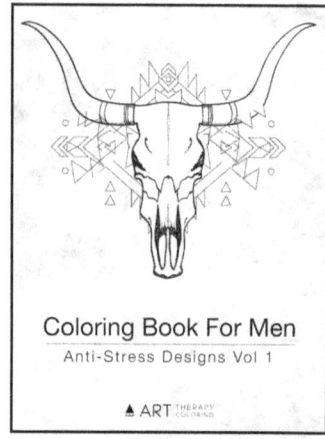

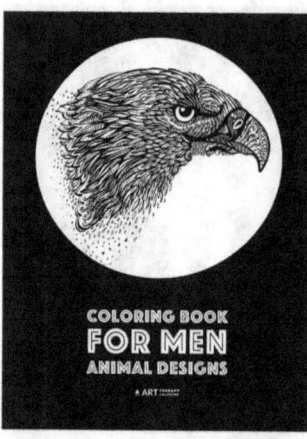

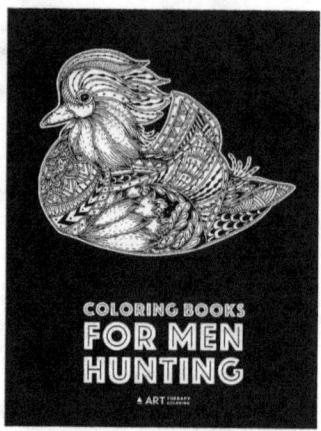

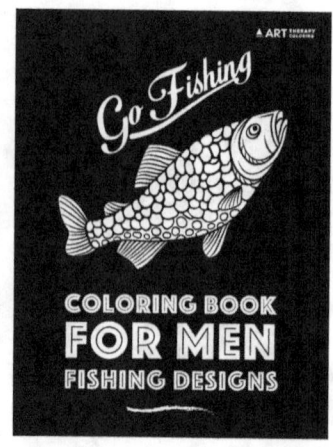

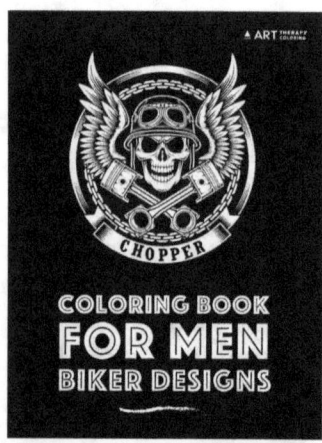

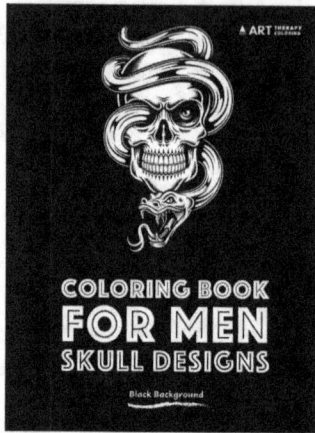

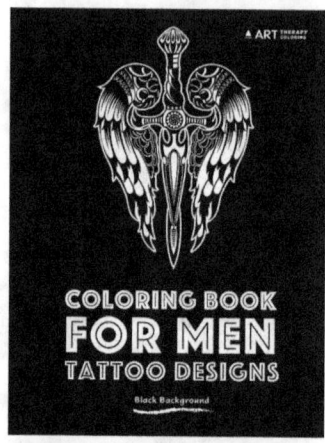

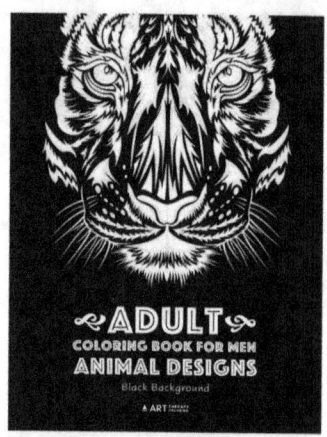

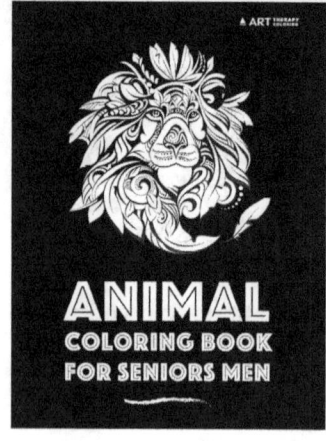

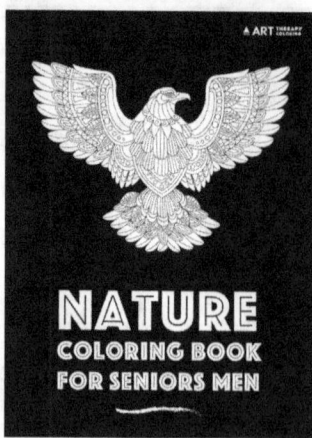

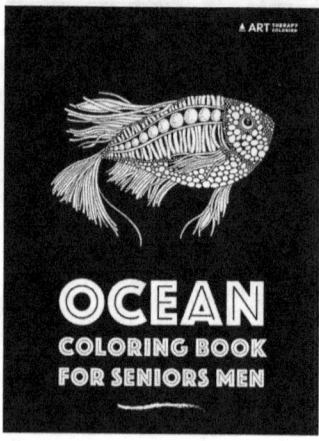

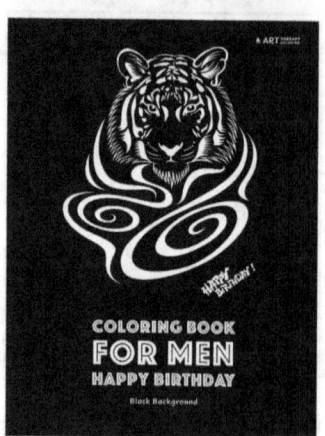

# Coloring Books For Seniors

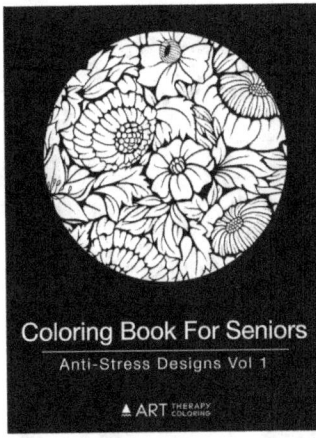

Coloring Book For Seniors
Anti-Stress Designs Vol 1

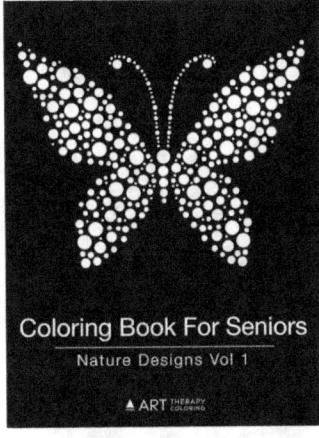

Coloring Book For Seniors
Nature Designs Vol 1

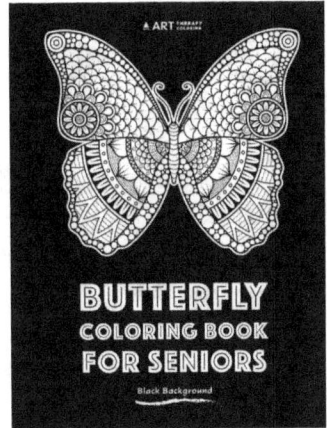

BUTTERFLY
COLORING BOOK
FOR SENIORS
Black Background

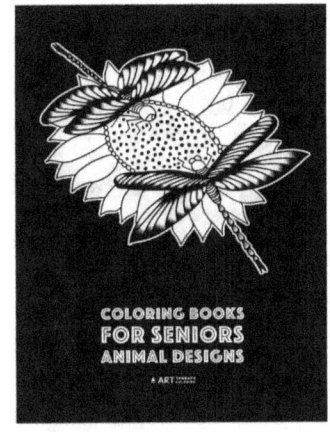

COLORING BOOKS
FOR SENIORS
ANIMAL DESIGNS

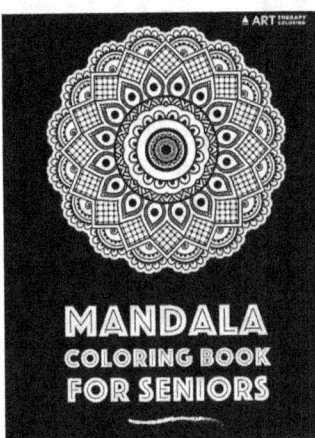

MANDALA
COLORING BOOK
FOR SENIORS

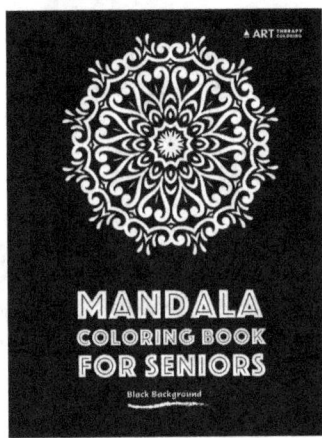

MANDALA
COLORING BOOK
FOR SENIORS
Black Background

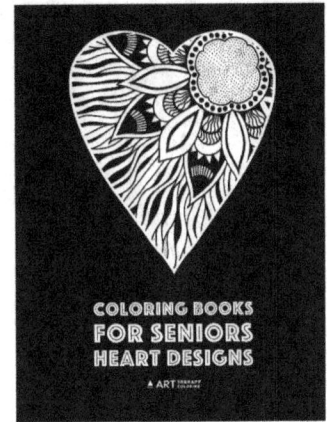

COLORING BOOKS
FOR SENIORS
HEART DESIGNS

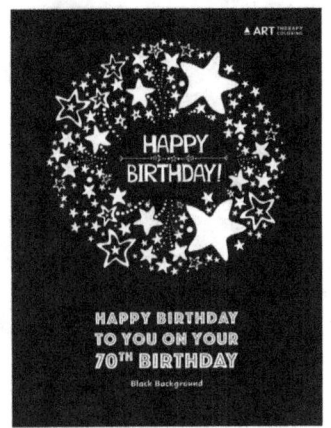

HAPPY BIRTHDAY
TO YOU ON YOUR
70TH BIRTHDAY
Black Background

COLORING BOOKS
FOR SENIORS
SWIRL DESIGNS
Black Background

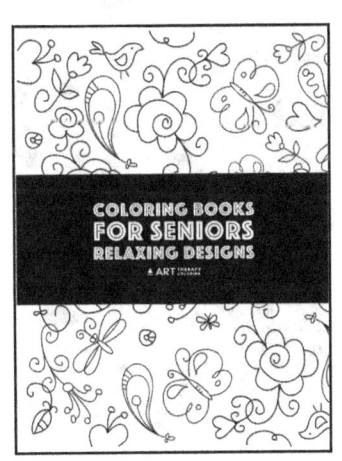

COLORING BOOKS
FOR SENIORS
RELAXING DESIGNS

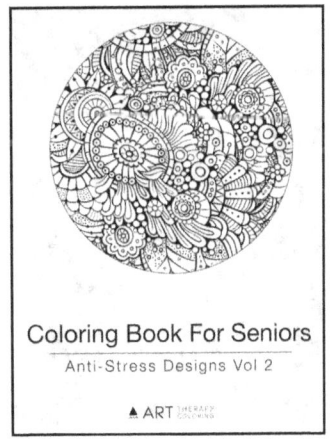

Coloring Book For Seniors
Anti-Stress Designs Vol 2

Coloring Book For Seniors
Anti-Stress Designs Vol 3

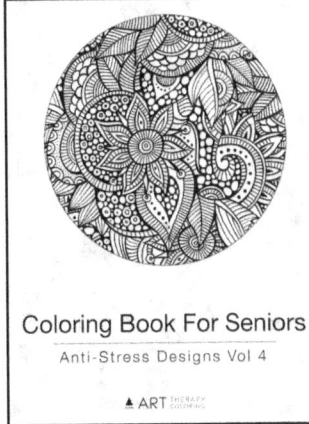

Coloring Book For Seniors
Anti-Stress Designs Vol 4

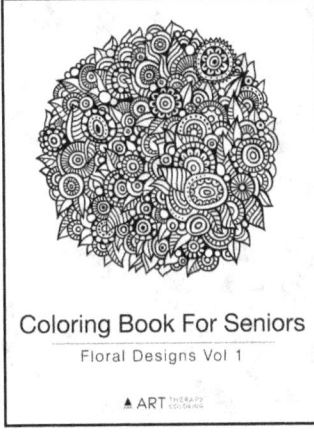

Coloring Book For Seniors
Floral Designs Vol 1

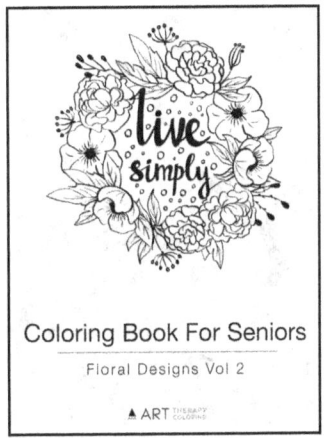

Coloring Book For Seniors
Floral Designs Vol 2

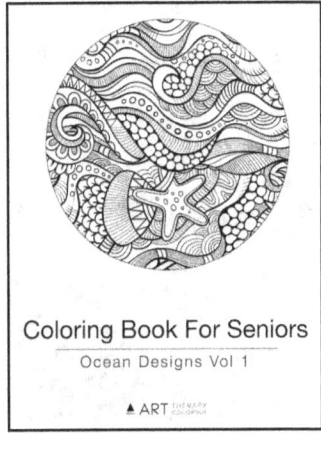

Coloring Book For Seniors
Ocean Designs Vol 1

# Coloring Books For Teens

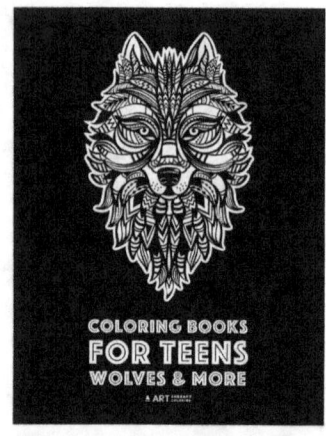

COLORING BOOKS
**FOR TEENS**
WOLVES & MORE

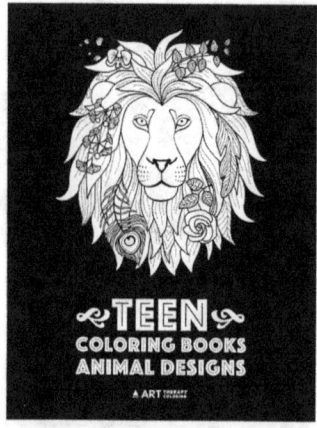

**TEEN**
COLORING BOOKS
ANIMAL DESIGNS

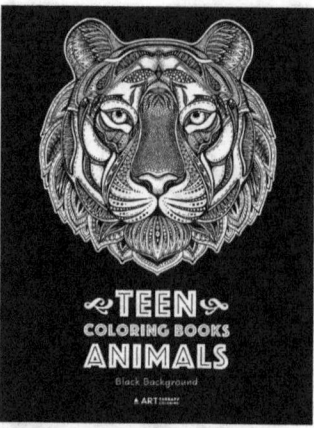

**TEEN**
COLORING BOOKS
**ANIMALS**
Black Background

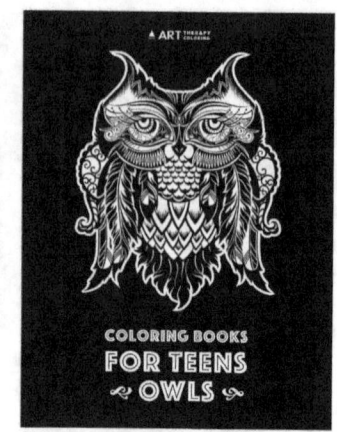

COLORING BOOKS
**FOR TEENS**
OWLS

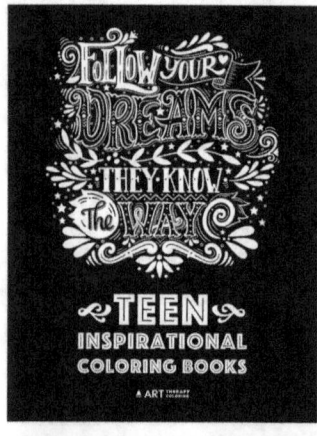

**TEEN**
INSPIRATIONAL
COLORING BOOKS

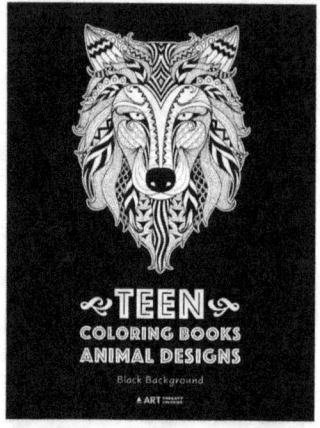

**TEEN**
COLORING BOOKS
ANIMAL DESIGNS
Black Background

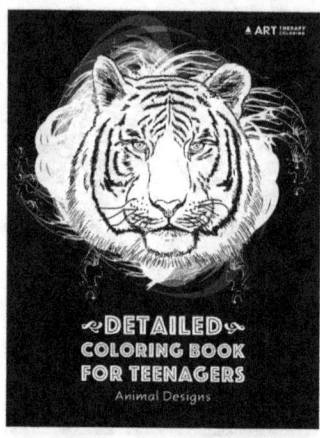

**DETAILED**
COLORING BOOK
FOR TEENAGERS
Animal Designs

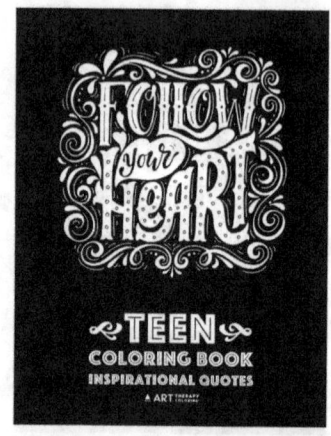

**TEEN**
COLORING BOOK
INSPIRATIONAL QUOTES

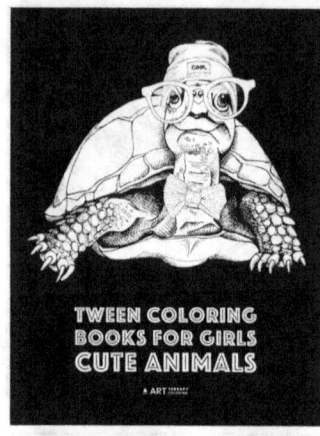

TWEEN COLORING
BOOKS FOR GIRLS
CUTE ANIMALS

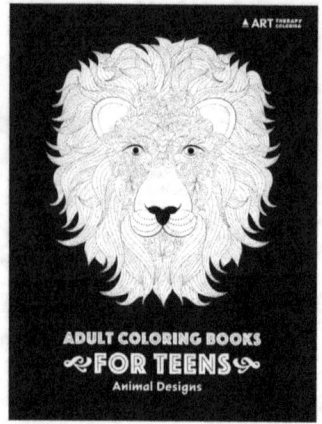

ADULT COLORING BOOKS
**FOR TEENS**
Animal Designs

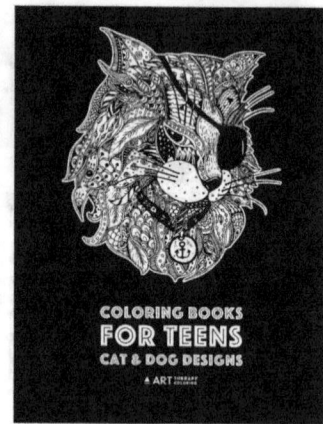

COLORING BOOKS
**FOR TEENS**
CAT & DOG DESIGNS

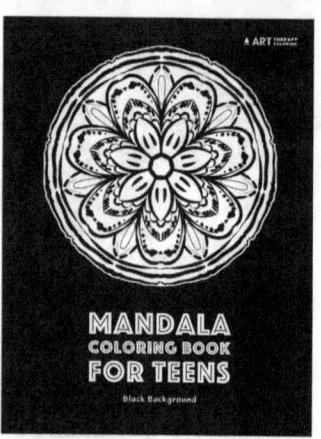

**MANDALA**
COLORING BOOK
**FOR TEENS**
Black Background

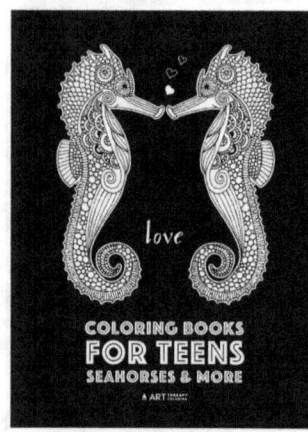

COLORING BOOKS
**FOR TEENS**
SEAHORSES & MORE

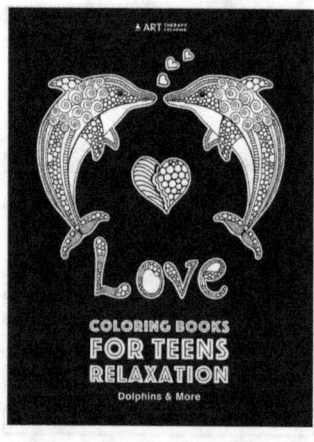

COLORING BOOKS
**FOR TEENS**
RELAXATION
Dolphins & More

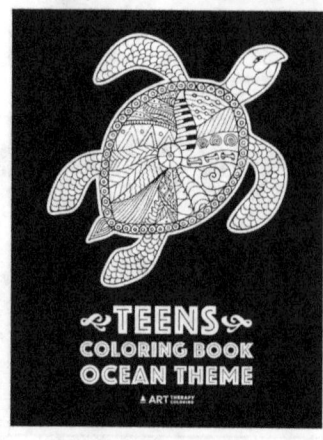

**TEENS**
COLORING BOOK
OCEAN THEME

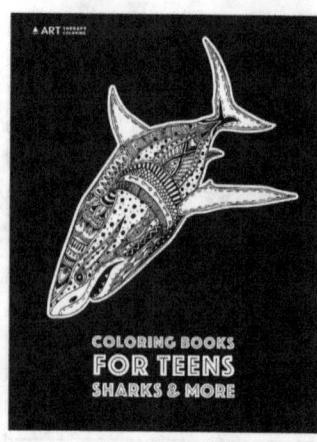

COLORING BOOKS
**FOR TEENS**
SHARKS & MORE

# Coloring Books For Teens

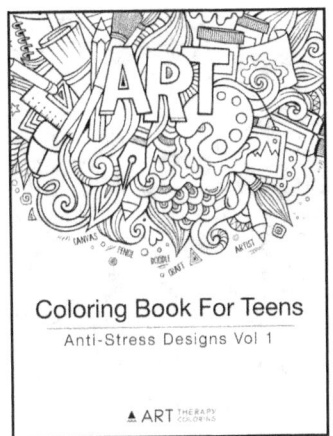

### Coloring Book For Teens
Anti-Stress Designs Vol 1

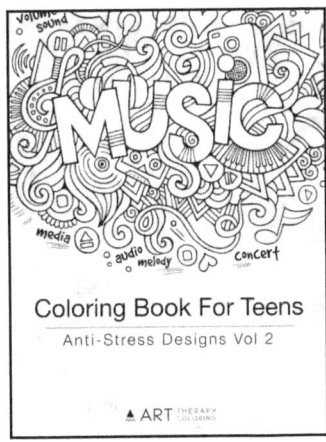

### Coloring Book For Teens
Anti-Stress Designs Vol 2

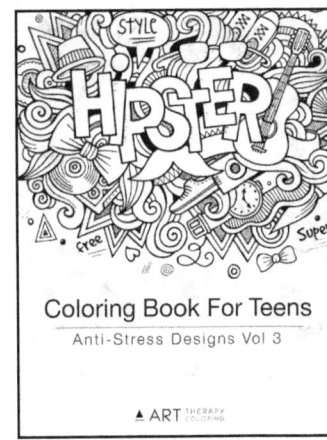

### Coloring Book For Teens
Anti-Stress Designs Vol 3

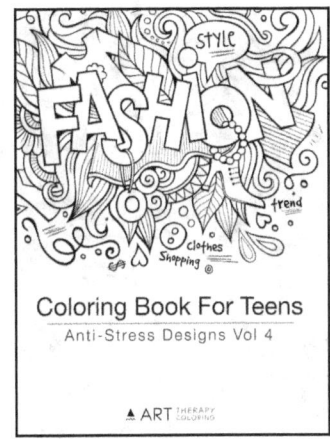

### Coloring Book For Teens
Anti-Stress Designs Vol 4

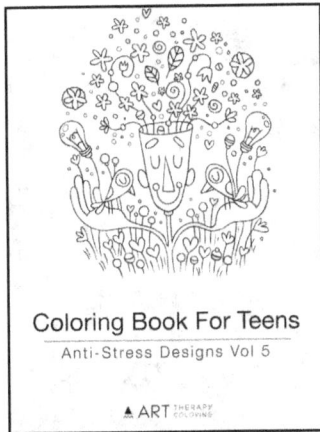

### Coloring Book For Teens
Anti-Stress Designs Vol 5

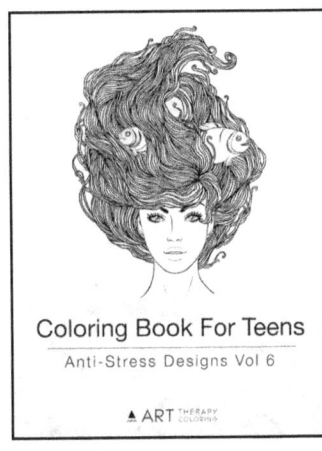

### Coloring Book For Teens
Anti-Stress Designs Vol 6

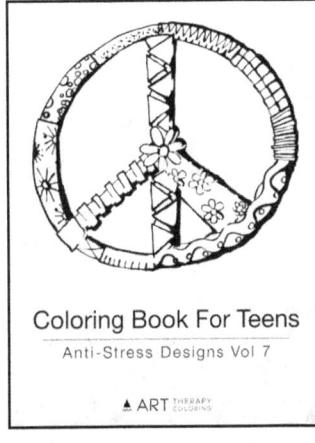

### Coloring Book For Teens
Anti-Stress Designs Vol 7

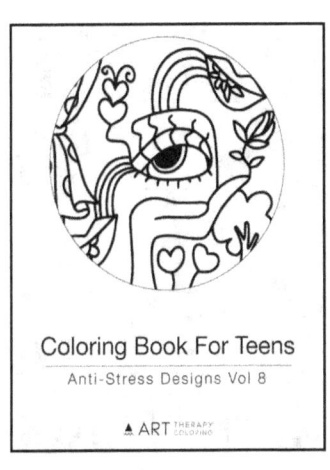

### Coloring Book For Teens
Anti-Stress Designs Vol 8

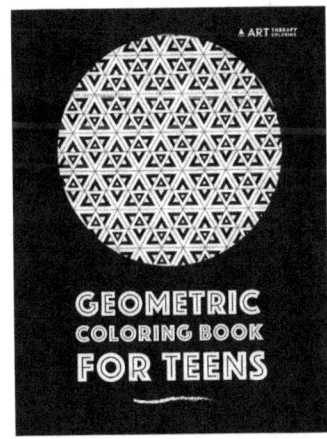

### GEOMETRIC COLORING BOOK FOR TEENS

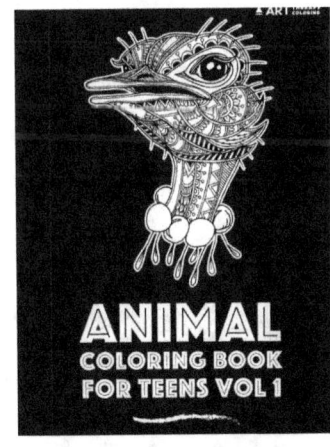

### ANIMAL COLORING BOOK FOR TEENS VOL 1

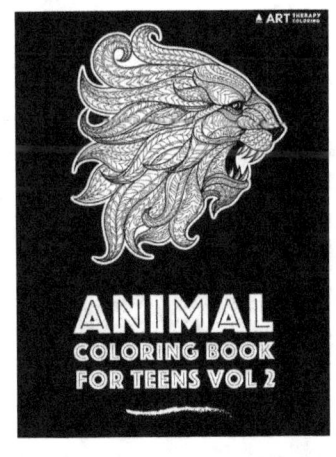

### ANIMAL COLORING BOOK FOR TEENS VOL 2

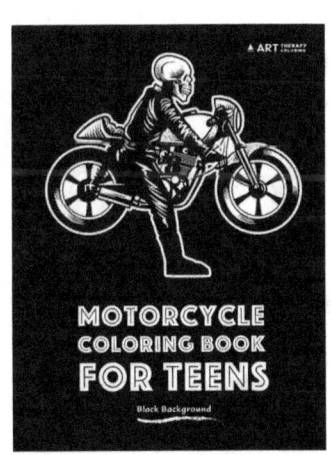

### MOTORCYCLE COLORING BOOK FOR TEENS
Black Background

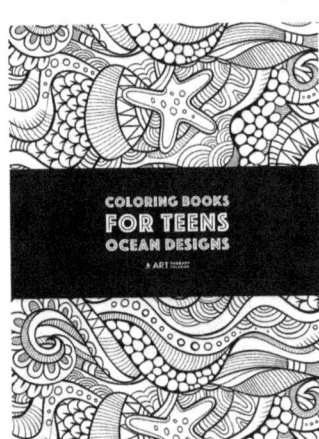

### COLORING BOOKS FOR TEENS OCEAN DESIGNS

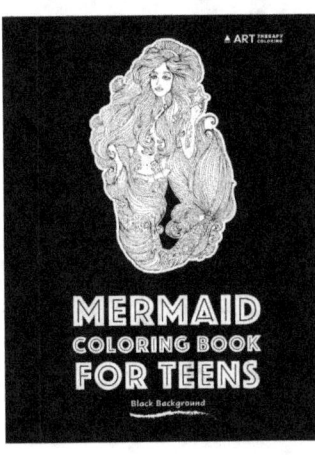

### MERMAID COLORING BOOK FOR TEENS
Black Background

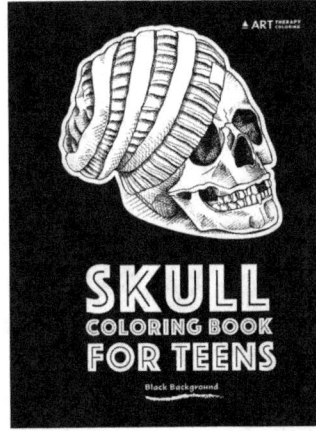

### SKULL COLORING BOOK FOR TEENS
Black Background

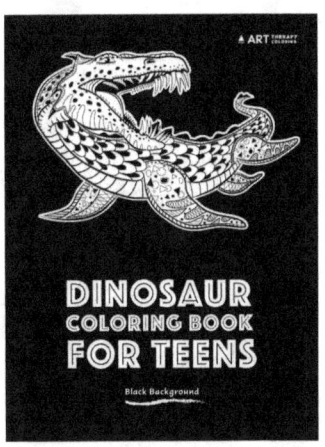

### DINOSAUR COLORING BOOK FOR TEENS
Black Background

# Coloring Books For Girls

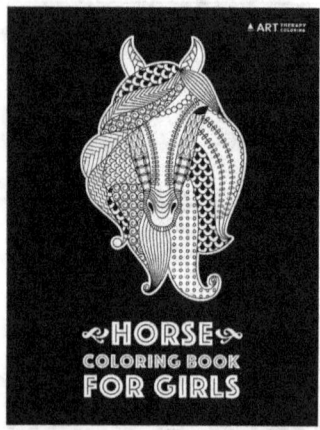

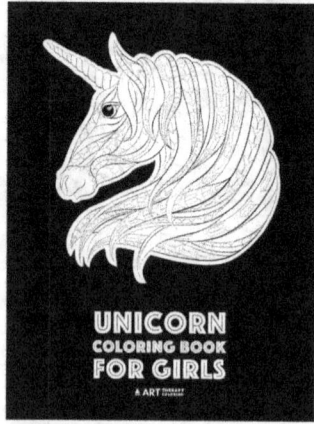

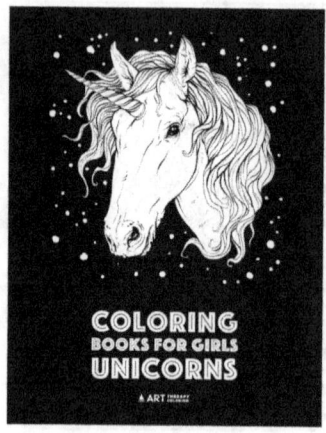

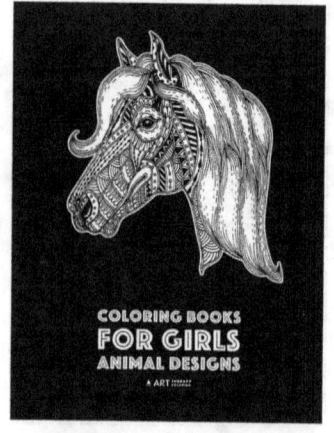

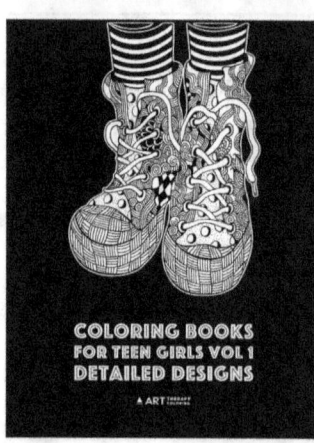

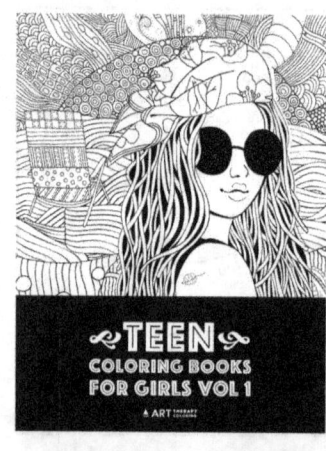

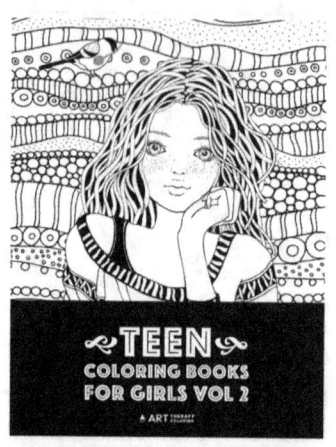

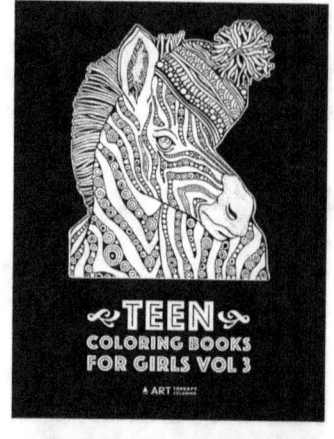

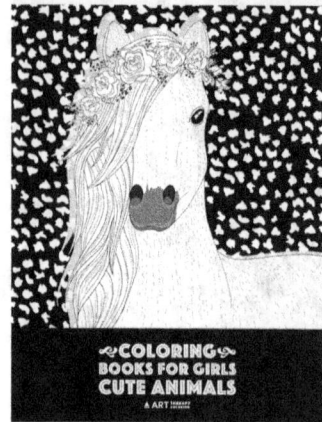

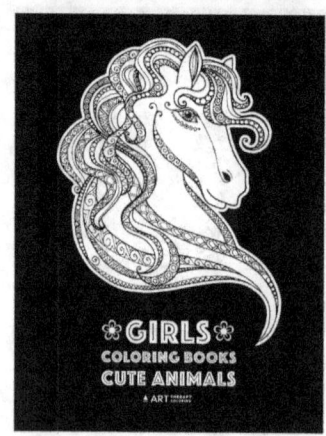

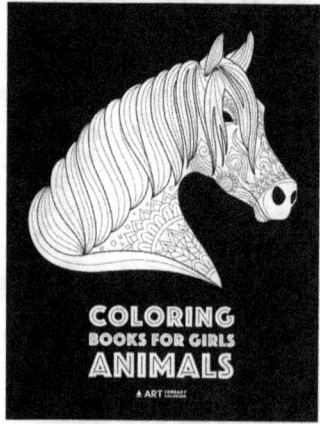

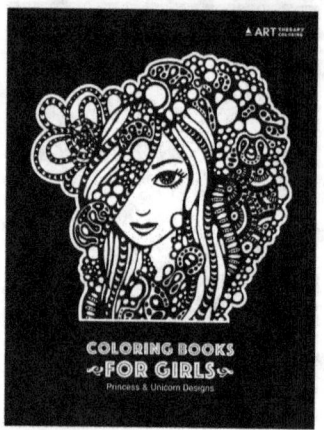

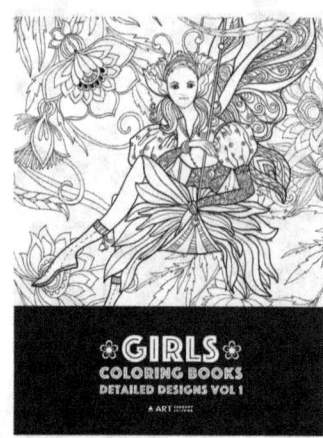

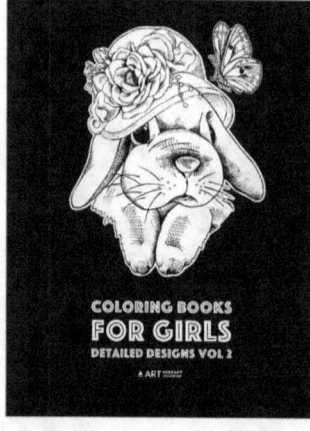

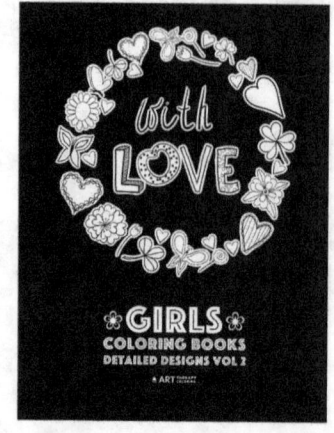

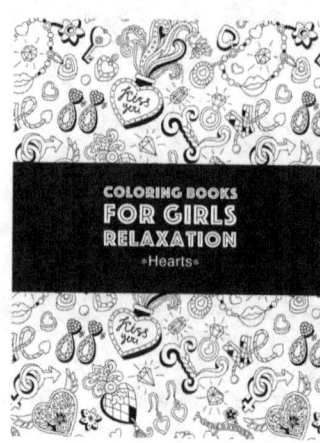

# Art Therapy Coloring Books

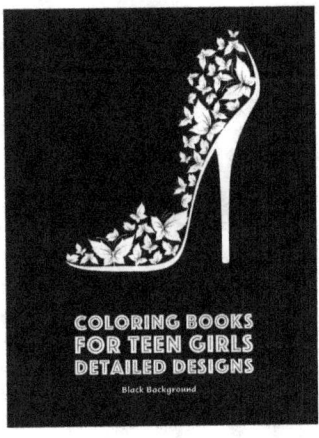

COLORING BOOKS
FOR TEEN GIRLS
DETAILED DESIGNS
Black Background

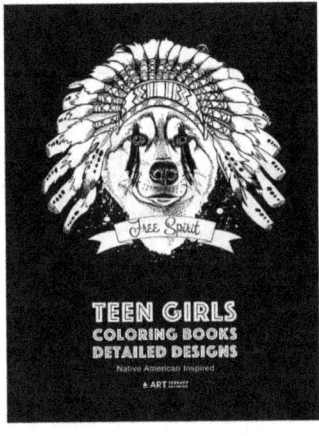

TEEN GIRLS
COLORING BOOKS
DETAILED DESIGNS
Native American Inspired
ART THERAPY COLORING

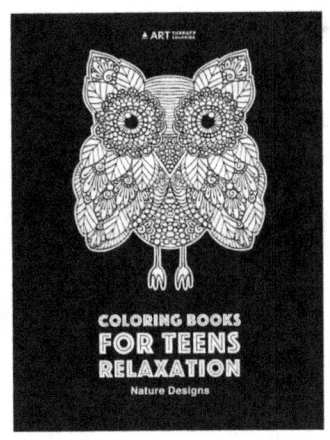

COLORING BOOKS
FOR TEENS
RELAXATION
Nature Designs

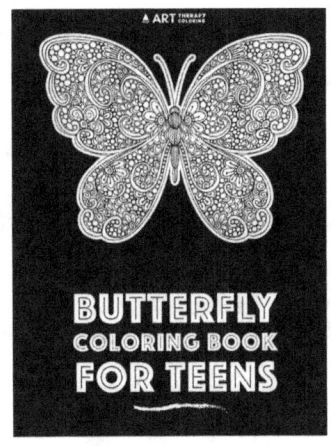

BUTTERFLY
COLORING BOOK
FOR TEENS

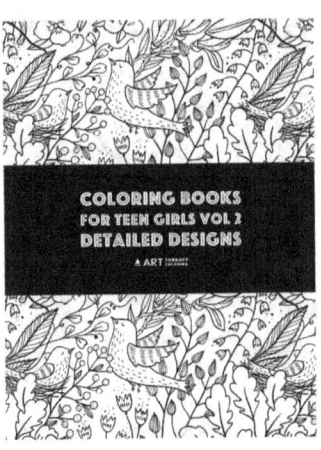

COLORING BOOKS
FOR TEEN GIRLS VOL 2
DETAILED DESIGNS
ART THERAPY COLORING

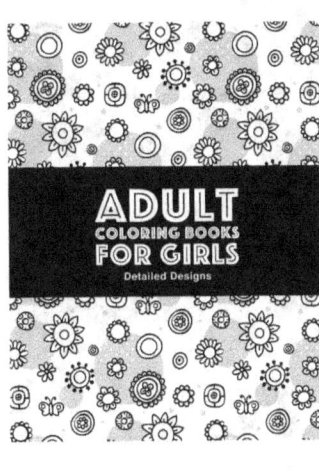

ADULT
COLORING BOOKS
FOR GIRLS
Detailed Designs

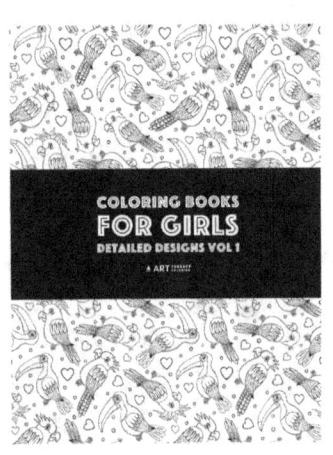

COLORING BOOKS
FOR GIRLS
DETAILED DESIGNS VOL 1
ART THERAPY COLORING

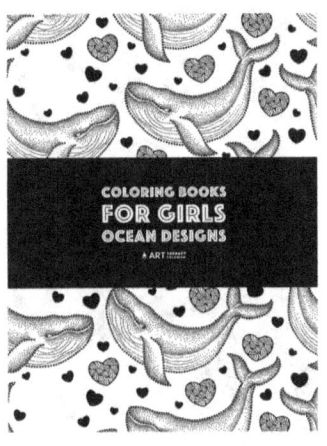

COLORING BOOKS
FOR GIRLS
OCEAN DESIGNS

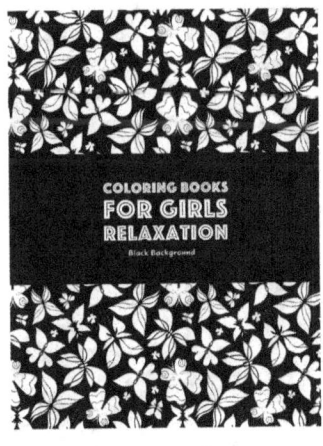

COLORING BOOKS
FOR GIRLS
RELAXATION
Black Background

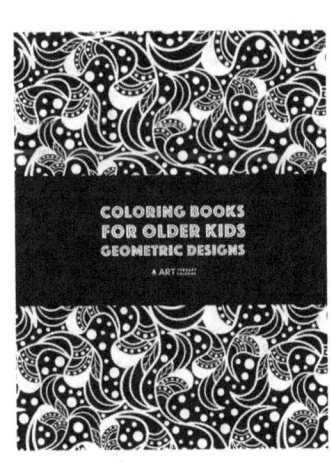

COLORING BOOKS
FOR OLDER KIDS
GEOMETRIC DESIGNS
ART THERAPY COLORING

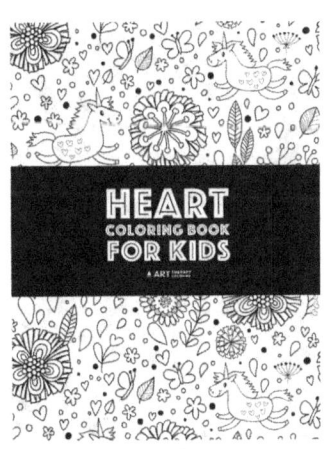

HEART
COLORING BOOK
FOR KIDS
ART THERAPY COLORING

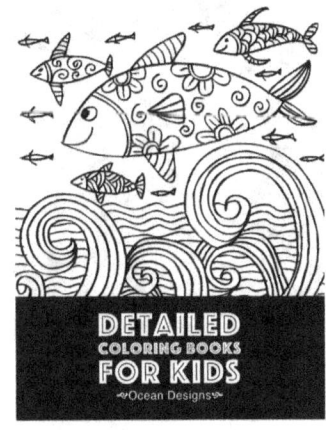

DETAILED
COLORING BOOKS
FOR KIDS
»Ocean Designs«

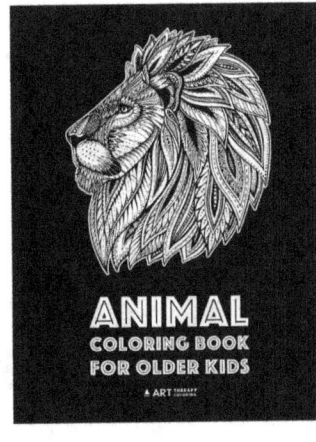

ANIMAL
COLORING BOOK
FOR OLDER KIDS
ART THERAPY COLORING

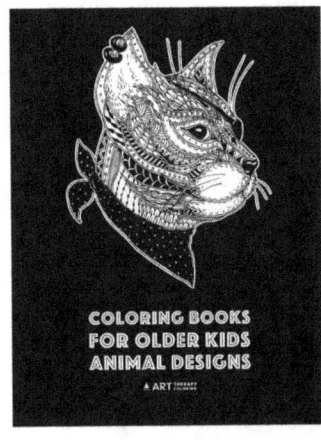

COLORING BOOKS
FOR OLDER KIDS
ANIMAL DESIGNS
ART THERAPY COLORING

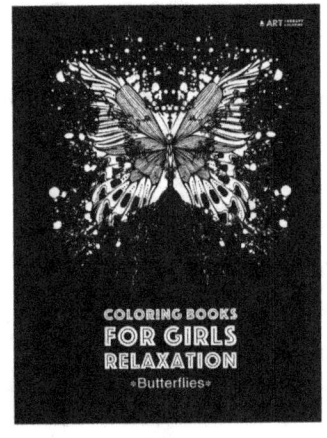

COLORING BOOKS
FOR GIRLS
RELAXATION
»Butterflies«

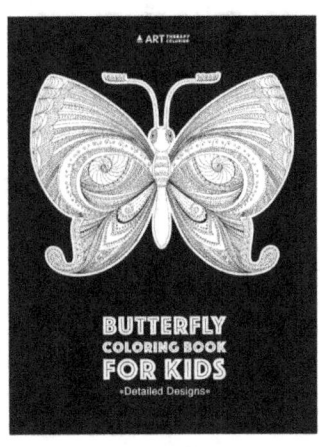

BUTTERFLY
COLORING BOOK
FOR KIDS
»Detailed Designs«
ART THERAPY COLORING

# Coloring Books For Boys

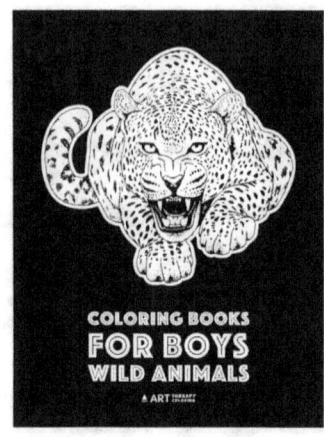

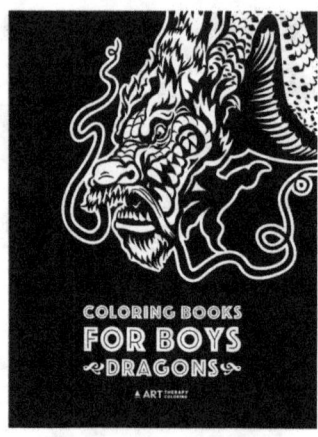

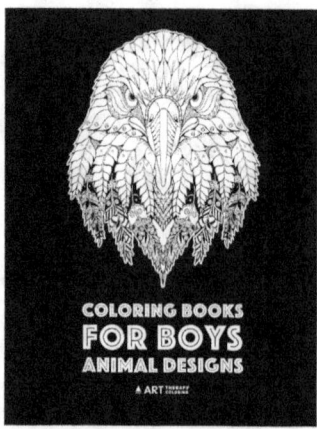

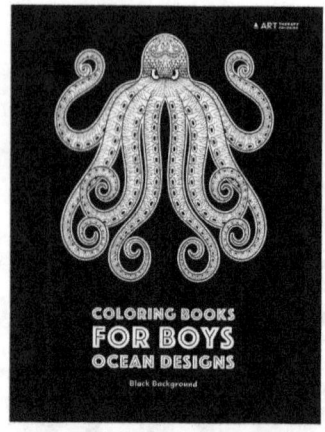

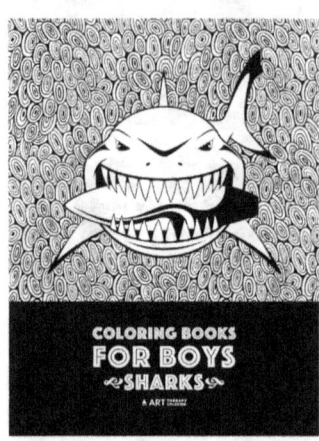

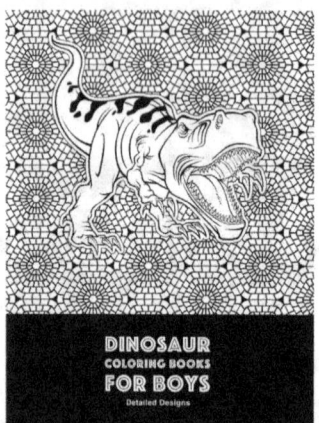

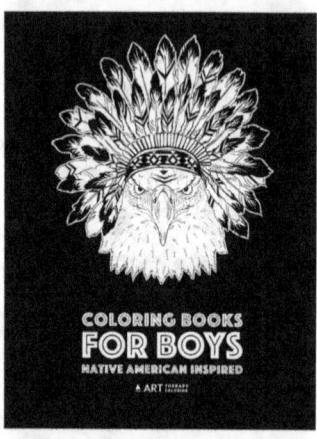

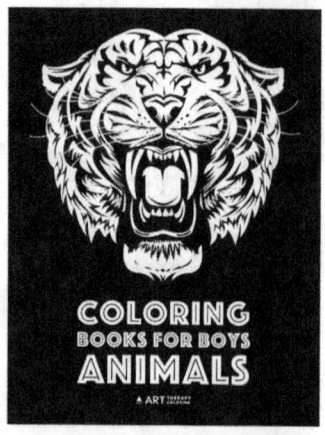

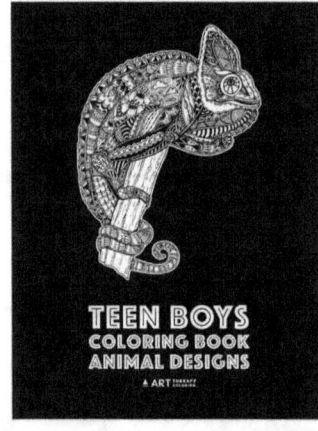

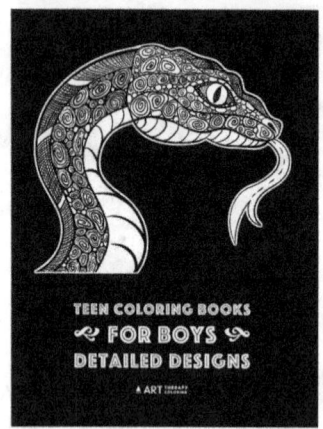

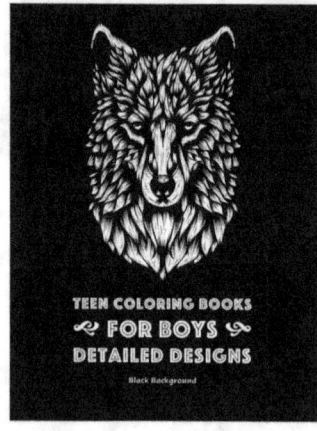

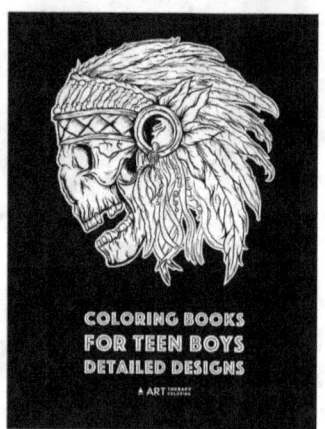

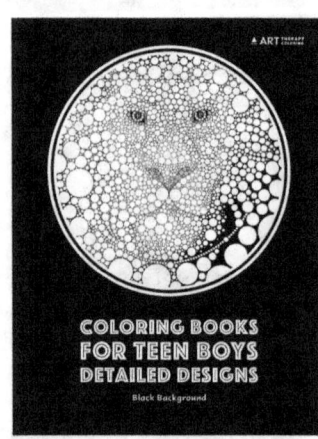

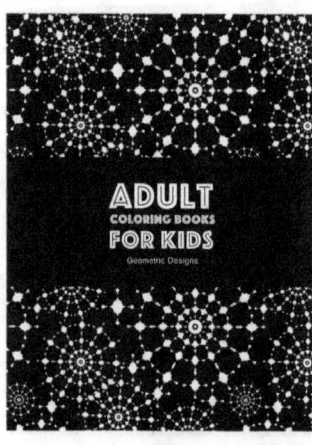

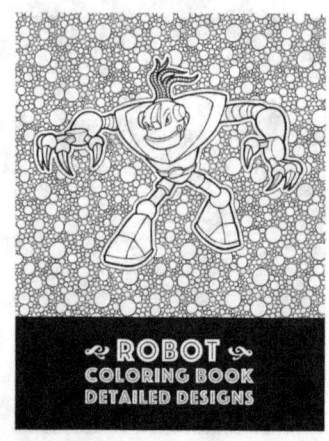

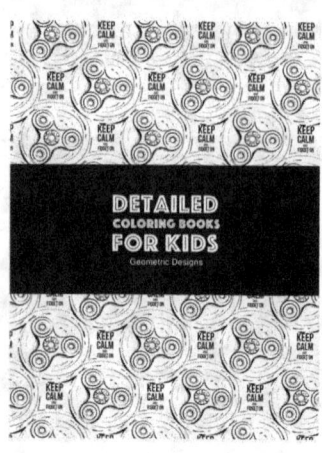

# Coloring Books For Kids

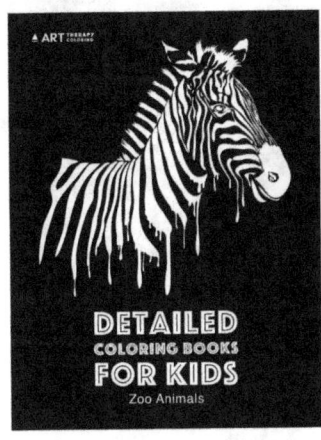

**DETAILED**
COLORING BOOKS
**FOR KIDS**
Zoo Animals

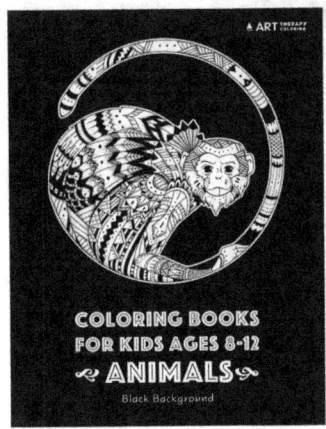

**COLORING BOOKS**
**FOR KIDS AGES 8-12**
**ANIMALS**
Black Background

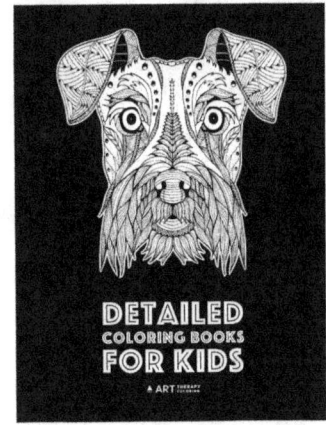

**DETAILED**
COLORING BOOKS
**FOR KIDS**

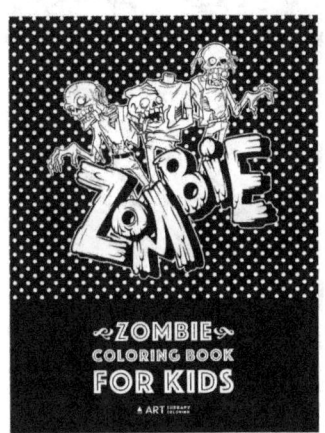

**ZOMBIE**
COLORING BOOK
**FOR KIDS**

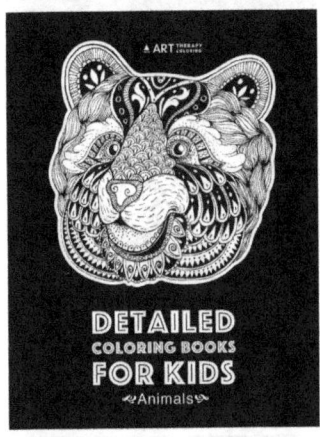

**DETAILED**
COLORING BOOKS
**FOR KIDS**
Animals

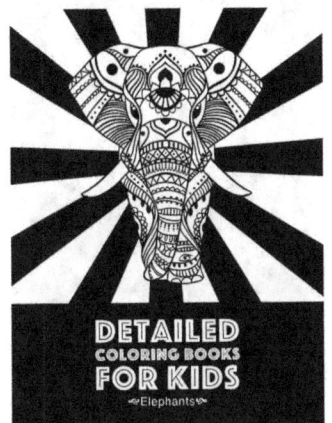

**DETAILED**
COLORING BOOKS
**FOR KIDS**
Elephants

**COLORING BOOKS**
**FOR KIDS**
OCEAN DESIGNS

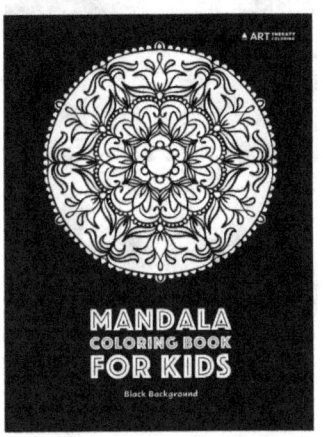

**MANDALA**
COLORING BOOK
**FOR KIDS**
Black Background

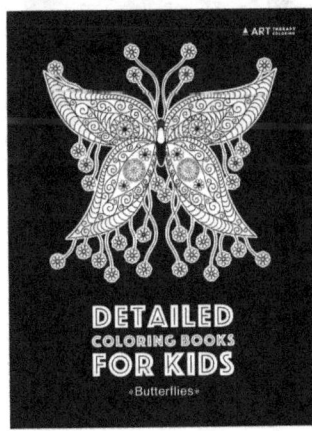

**DETAILED**
COLORING BOOKS
**FOR KIDS**
Butterflies

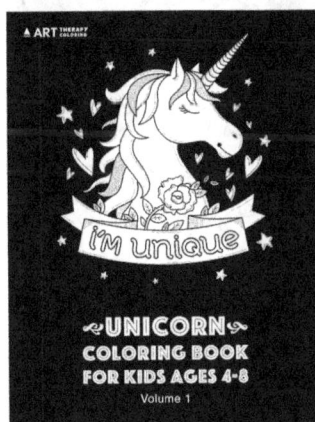

**UNICORN**
COLORING BOOK
**FOR KIDS AGES 4-8**
Volume 1

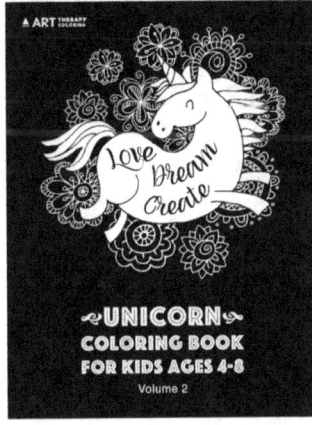

**UNICORN**
COLORING BOOK
**FOR KIDS AGES 4-8**
Volume 2

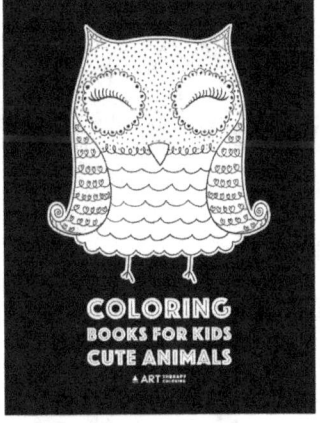

**COLORING**
BOOKS FOR KIDS
CUTE ANIMALS

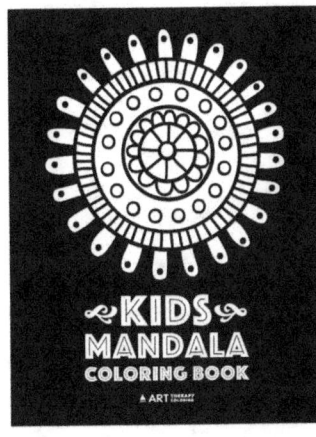

**KIDS**
**MANDALA**
COLORING BOOK

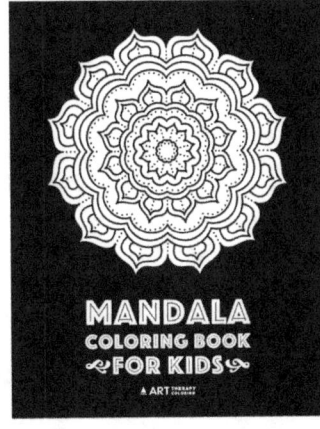

**MANDALA**
COLORING BOOK
**FOR KIDS**

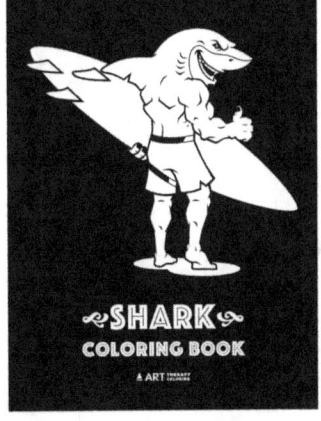

**SHARK**
COLORING BOOK

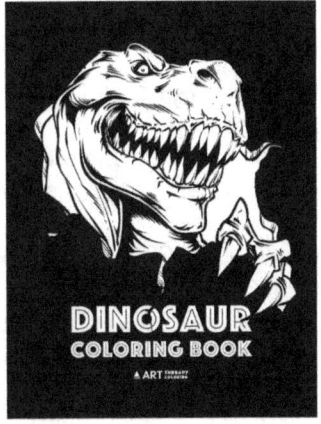

**DINOSAUR**
COLORING BOOK

# Coloring Books For Special Occasions

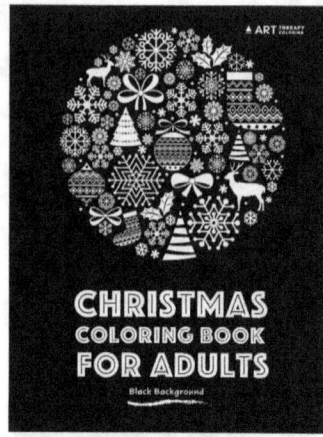
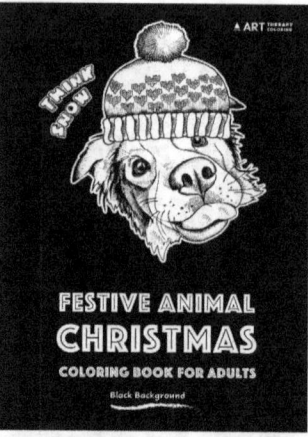
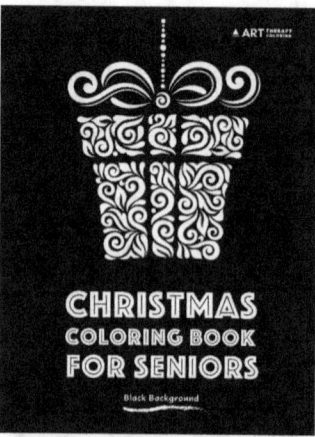
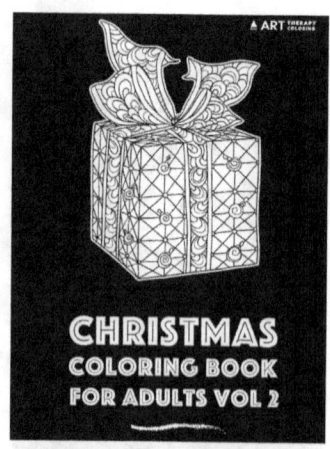

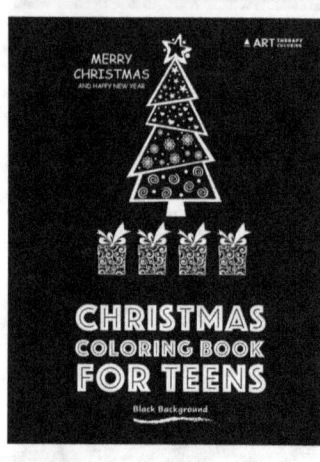
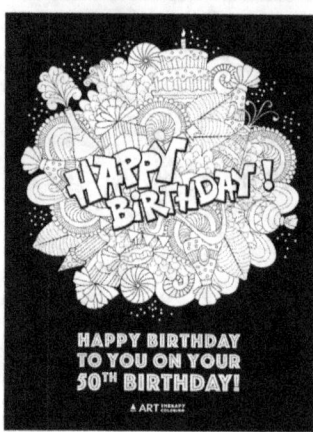
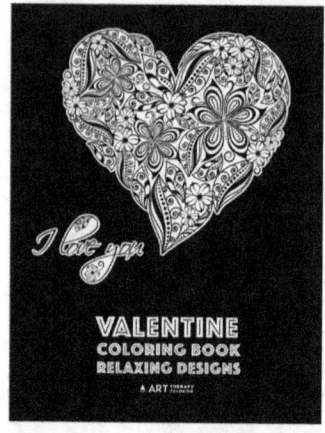
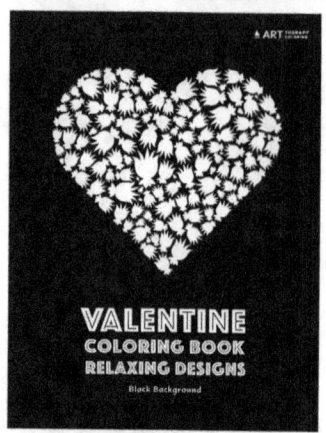

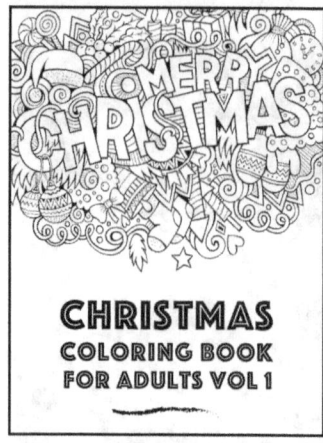
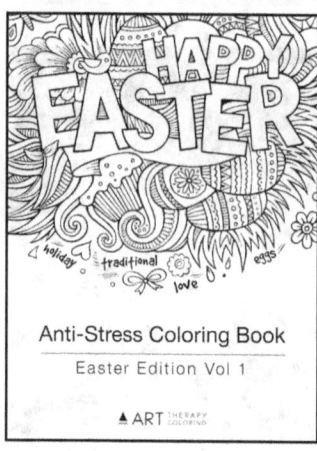
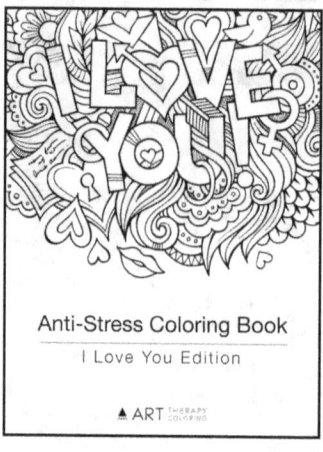
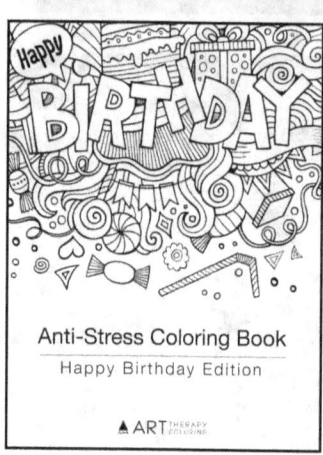

Tiger Coloring Book For Adults

Published by:
Art Therapy Coloring
El Dorado Hills, California
www.arttherapycoloring.com

Shutterstock Images

ISBN: 978-1-64126-023-7